The 52 Week Movie Challenge

Compiled by

Christian Beecham

DEDICATION

For Mum and Dad, who bought this movie-obsessed
teenager his first VCR all those years ago.

Welcome, to Movie Challenge Club:

1. The first rule of Movie Challenge Club is you must talk about Movie Challenge Club.
2. The second rule of Movie Challenge Club is YOU MUST TALK ABOUT MOVIE CHALLENGE CLUB!
3. You can take as long as you want to complete the challenges. We suggest a challenge a week but do them at your own pace.
4. Challenges can be done in any order.
5. You *could* watch 1 movie to complete multiple. challenges. We won't stop you, but don't expect a round of applause.
6. You *could* re-watch a movie to complete a challenge however, we encourage you to watch a movie you've never seen before. If you're going to re-watch a movie, watch a movie you've only seen once, and a long time ago (in a galaxy far far away).
7. On some challenges we've provided some recommendations of movies that meet the challenge but watch any movie you feel meets the criteria. Seeking recommendations from friends/social media is a great place to start.

Are you ready? Let's Begin…

The Challenges

- ☐ 1. Single Word Title
- ☐ 2. Set in the Future
- ☐ 3. A Famous Actor's Early Work
- ☐ 4. Based on a Short Story
- ☐ 5. Directed by a Woman
- ☐ 6. An Odd Couple
- ☐ 7. The 1990s
- ☐ 8. Best Picture Winner
- ☐ 9. Animated
- ☐ 10. A Feature-Length Documentary
- ☐ 11. A Current or Previous Crush
- ☐ 12. Black and White
- ☐ 13. English Language, Foreign Director
- ☐ 14. Place Name in the Title
- ☐ 15. Based on Comic/Graphic Novel
- ☐ 16. Starring Blood Relatives
- ☐ 17. A Musical
- ☐ 18. Creature Feature
- ☐ 19. Foreign Movie
- ☐ 20. Set on a Vehicle
- ☐ 21. When I grow up, I want to be…
- ☐ 22. The Title Contains a Number
- ☐ 23. An Epic
- ☐ 24. A Silent Movie
- ☐ 25. Crime
- ☐ 26. Disaster Movie

- ☐ 27. Released by A24
- ☐ 28. Favourite Director
- ☐ 29. Non-Human Protagonist/Antagonist
- ☐ 30. Show Me the Money
- ☐ 31. Whodunnit
- ☐ 32. Titular Character
- ☐ 33. Stop Motion Animation
- ☐ 34. Set in a Location You Love
- ☐ 35. Historic War
- ☐ 36. Stephen King Adaptation
- ☐ 37. Jaw-Dropping Cinematography
- ☐ 38. An Obsession
- ☐ 39. Powerful Endings
- ☐ 40. A Movie the Same Age as You
- ☐ 41. LGBTQIA+
- ☐ 42. The Title is a Question
- ☐ 43. Film Noir
- ☐ 44. A Title at Least 5 Words Long
- ☐ 45. Doesn't Take Place on Earth
- ☐ 46. 25, 50 or 100 Year Anniversary
- ☐ 47. Set in the Winter
- ☐ 48. Biggest Return on Investment
- ☐ 49. One Actor, Multiple Roles
- ☐ 50. Based on a Video Game
- ☐ 51. A Christmas Movie
- ☐ 52. Released This Year

Single Word Title

Let's start your movie challenge journey with an easy one.
Watch a movie with a title compromising of a single word.
No "The ..." or "A ...", no spaces or hyphens.

Movie Watched:

_____

Directed By: Year Released:

_____   _____

Starring: Date Completed:

_____   _____

Your Review

_____

_____

_____

_____   ☆ ☆ ☆ ☆ ☆

Would you recommend it, and if so to who?

_____

_____

Using at least 5 words, give the movie a new title:

_____

_____

Here are some recommendations to get you started.
Don't forget to ask friends for their recommendations!

Action

- ☐ Rififi (1955)
- ☐ Django (1966)
- ☐ Dual (1971)
- ☐ Ran (1985)
- ☐ Platoon (1986)
- ☐ Ran (1985)
- ☐ Subramaniapuram (2008)
- ☐ Watchmen (2009)
- ☐ Dunkirk (2017)
- ☐ Tenet (2021)

Comedy

- ☐ Sabrina (1954)
- ☐ M*A*S*H (1970)
- ☐ Airplane! (1980)
- ☐ Clue (1985)
- ☐ Heathers (1989)
- ☐ Clerks (1994)
- ☐ Rushmore (1998)
- ☐ Adaptation (2002)
- ☐ Booksmart (2019)
- ☐ Soul (2020)

Drama

- ☐ M (1931)
- ☐ Casablanca (1942)
- ☐ Yojimbo (1961)
- ☐ Chinatown (1974)
- ☐ Rocky (1976)
- ☐ Amadeus (1984)
- ☐ Magnolia (1999)
- ☐ Drive (2011)
- ☐ Boyhood (2014)
- ☐ Minari (2020)

Horror

- ☐ Frankenstein (1931)
- ☐ THEM! (1954)
- ☐ Diabolique (1955)
- ☐ Psycho (1960)
- ☐ Suspiria (1977)
- ☐ Possession (1981)
- ☐ Audition (1999)
- ☐ Orphan (2009)
- ☐ Midsommer (2019)
- ☐ Malignant (2021)

Romance

- ☐ Casablanca (1942)
- ☐ Marty (1955)
- ☐ Charade (1963)
- ☐ Cabaret (1972)
- ☐ Reds (1981)
- ☐ Mermaids (1990)
- ☐ Titanic (1997)
- ☐ Amelie (2001)
- ☐ Her (2013)
- ☐ Emma (2020)

Thriller

- ☐ Fury (1936)
- ☐ Gaslight (1944)
- ☐ Vertigo (1958)
- ☐ Sorcerer (1974)
- ☐ Manhunter (1986)
- ☐ Heat (1995)
- ☐ Cube (1997)
- ☐ Oldboy (2003)
- ☐ Argo (2012)
- ☐ Titane (2021)

Set in the Future

For this challenge, you should watch a film set in the future. While watching consider how accurate you think the depiction of the future is.

Movie Watched:

_____

Directed By: Year Released:

_____   _____

Starring: Date Completed:

_____   _____

Your Review

_____

_____

_____

_____

_____   ☆ ☆ ☆ ☆ ☆

Would you recommend it, and if so to who?

_____

_____

Do think the future depiction will turn out to be accurate?

_____

_____

These movies are all set in the future. You can find more by searching "movies set in the future" on the internet.

Near (Set in the year 20xx)

- ☐ Her (2013)
- ☐ Children of Men (2006)
- ☐ Snowpiercer (2013)
- ☐ I, Robot (2004)
- ☐ Meet the Robinsons (2007)
- ☐ Isle of Dogs (2018)
- ☐ The Book of Eli (2010)
- ☐ Looper (2012)
- ☐ Ready Player One (2018)
- ☐ Doom (2005)
- ☐ Event Horizon (1997)
- ☐ Blade Runner 2049 (2017)
- ☐ Minority Report (2002)
- ☐ Sunshine (2007)
- ☐ Interstellar (2014)
- ☐ Lockout (2012)
- ☐ Total Recall (1990)
- ☐ The Hunger Games (2012)
- ☐ Enemy Mine (1985)
- ☐ Prometheus (2012)

Far (Set in the year 2100+)

- ☐ Forbidden Planet (1956)
- ☐ Barbarella (1968)
- ☐ Dune (1984, 2021)
- ☐ Nausicaä of the Valley of the Wind (1984)
- ☐ Star Trek (1979, 2009)
- ☐ THX 1138 (1971)
- ☐ Logan's Run (1976)
- ☐ The Black Hole (1979)
- ☐ Alien (1979)
- ☐ The Fifth Element (1997)
- ☐ Pitch Black (2000)
- ☐ Idiocracy (2006)
- ☐ A.I. Artificial Intelligence (2001)
- ☐ Astro Boy (2009)
- ☐ Dredd (2012)
- ☐ Cloud Atlas (2012)
- ☐ Alita: Battle Angel (2019)
- ☐ Ad Astra (2019)

Whenever they are (No exact year specified)

- ☐ Fahrenheit 451 (1966, 2018)
- ☐ Solaris (1972, 2002)
- ☐ Silent Running (1972)
- ☐ Saturn 3 (1980)
- ☐ Outland (1981)
- ☐ Le Dernier Combat (1983)
- ☐ Brazil (1985)
- ☐ Prayer of the Rollerboys (1990)
- ☐ Ghost in the Shell (1995)
- ☐ Gattaca (1997)
- ☐ eXistenZ (1999)
- ☐ Treasure Planet (2002)
- ☐ The Final Cut (2004)
- ☐ The Maze Runner (2014)
- ☐ Downsizing (2017)
- ☐ Life (2017)
- ☐ Upgrade (2018)
- ☐ Mute (2018)
- ☐ Mortal Engines (2018)

A Famous Actor's Early Work

Barring the lucky(?) few, we all start a career on the bottom rung of the ladder, and actors are no exception. Choose an actor and watch one of their first 3 movies.

Movie Watched:

_____

Directed By: Year Released:

_____   _____

Starring: Date Completed:

_____   _____

Your Review

_____

_____

_____

_____

_____   ☆ ☆ ☆ ☆ ☆

Would you recommend it, and if so to who?

_____

_____

Did the actor show any traits you now find familiar to them?

_____

_____

A few suggestions are listed below. Look up actors you enjoy on IMDB and see which early work entices you.

- ☐ Seed (1931)   – *Betty Davis*
- ☐ This is the Night (1932)   – *Cary Grant*
- ☐ A Bill of Divorcement (1932)   – *Katharine Hepburn*
- ☐ The Murder Man (1935)   – *James Stewart*
- ☐ The Farmer Takes a Wife (1935)   – *Henry Fonda*
- ☐ Captain Blood (1935)   – *Errol Flynn*
- ☐ Tower of London (1939)   – *Vincent Price*
- ☐ Lassie Come Home (1943)   – *Elizabeth Taylor*
- ☐ The Shocking Miss Pilgrim (1947)   – *Marilyn Monroe*
- ☐ The Men (1950)   – *Marlon Brando*
- ☐ No Wat Out (1950)   – *Sidney Poitier*
- ☐ The Lavender Hill Mob (1951)   – *Audrey Hepburn*
- ☐ The Trouble with Harry (1955)   – *Shirley MacLaine*
- ☐ The Little Shop of Horrors (1960)   – *Jack Nicholson*
- ☐ The Pawnbroker (1964)   – *Morgan Freeman*
- ☐ Three Rooms in Manhattan (1965)   – *Robert De Niro*
- ☐ Hercules in New York (1970)   – *Arnold Schwarzenegger*
- ☐ The Panic in Needle Park (1971)   – *Al Pacino*
- ☐ Julia (1977)   – *Meryl Streep*
- ☐ Midnight Madness (1980)   – *Michael J. Fox*
- ☐ Taps (1981)   – *Tom Cruise*
- ☐ Labyrinth of Passion (1982)   – *Antonio Banderas*
- ☐ 48 Hours (1982)   – *Eddie Murphy*
- ☐ Blood Simple (1984)   – *Frances McDormand*
- ☐ Yes, Madam! (1985)   – *Michelle Yeoh*
- ☐ Return to Horror High (1987)   – *George Clooney*
- ☐ Mystic Pizza (1988)   – *Matt Damon*
- ☐ Critters 3 (1991)   – *Leonardo DiCaprio*
- ☐ Jungle Fever (1991)   – *Halle Berry*
- ☐ Roadracers (1994)   – *Salma Hayek*
- ☐ 2 Days in the Valley (1996)   – *Charlize Theron*
- ☐ Primal Fear (1996)   – *Edward Norton*
- ☐ Leon (1994)   – *Natalie Portman*
- ☐ Hardball (2001)   – *Michael B. Jordan*
- ☐ Superbad (2007)   – *Emma Stone*
- ☐ True Grit (2010)   – *Hailee Steinfeld*

Based on a Short Story

Adapting a novel to a movie usually results in parts left out.
However, short stories are perfect for movie adaptations.
This challenge is to watch a movie based on a short story.

Movie Watched:

_____

Directed By: Year Released:

_____   _____

Starring: Date Completed:

_____   _____

Your Review

_____

_____

_____

_____   ☆ ☆ ☆ ☆ ☆

Would you recommend it, and if so to who?

_____

_____

Have you read the story? If not, will you?

_____

_____

The films below are all equal to or surpass the original short story – which is also worth a read.

- ☐ Mr. Deeds Goes to Town (1936), Mr Deeds (2002)
  - "Opera Hat", Clarence Budington Kelland
- ☐ It's a Wonderful Life (1946)
  - "The Greatest Gift", Philip Van Doren Stern
- ☐ The Day the Earth Stood Still (1951, 2008)
  - "Farewell to the Master", Harry Bates
- ☐ The Thing from Another World (1951), The Thing (1982)
  - "Who Goes There?" John W. Campbell Jr.
- ☐ A Face in the Crowd (1957)
  - "Your Arkansas Traveler", Budd Schulberg
- ☐ The Fly (1958, 1986)
  - "The Fly", George Langelaan
- ☐ Breakfast at Tiffany's (1961)
  - "Breakfast at Tiffany's", Truman Capote
- ☐ The Swimmer (1968)
  - "The Swimmer", John Cheever
- ☐ Don't Look Now (1973)
  "Not After Midnight" Daphne du Maurier
- ☐ The Duellists (1977)
  "The Duel", Joseph Conrad
- ☐ Stand By Me (1986)
  - "The Body", Stephen King
- ☐ Hellraiser (1987)
  - "The Hellbound Heart", Clive Barker
- ☐ Total Recall (1990, 2012)
  - "We Can Remember It for You Wholesale", Philip K. Dick
- ☐ The Shawshank Redemption (1994)
  - "Rita Hayworth and Shawshank Redemption", Stephen King
- ☐ Bicentennial Man (1999)
  - "The Bicentennial Man", Isaac Asmimov
- ☐ Secretary (2002)
  - "Secretary", Mary Gaitskill
- ☐ Brokeback Mountain (2005)
  - "Brokeback Mountain", Annie Proulx
- ☐ Real Steel (2011)
  - "Steel", Richard Matheson

Directed by a Woman

Every year more women are making their breakthrough directing movies. It's time to celebrate movies directed by women, pick one for this challenge.

Movie Watched:

_____

Directed By: Year Released:

_____   _____

Starring: Date Completed:

_____   _____

Your Review

_____

_____

_____

_____   ☆ ☆ ☆ ☆ ☆

Would you recommend it, and if so to who?

_____

_____

Will you seek out more movies by this director?

_____

_____

Here is a small list to get you started. It's also worth looking up each director below to see their other movies.

- ☐ Cléo from 5 to 7 (1962)   *- Agnes Varda*
- ☐ Mikey and Nicky (1976)   *- Elaine May*
- ☐ Losing Ground (1982)   *- Kathleen Collins*
- ☐ Yentl (1983)   *- Barbra Streisand*
- ☐ Desperately Seeking Susan (1985)   *- Susan Seidelman*
- ☐ Near Dark (1987)   *- Kathryn Bigelow*
- ☐ Awakenings (1990)   *- Penny Marshall*
- ☐ Rambling Rose (1991)   *- Martha Coolidge*
- ☐ The Piano (1993)   *- Jane Campion*
- ☐ The Secret Garden (1993)   *- Agnieszka Holland*
- ☐ Clueless (1995)   *- Amy Heckerling*
- ☐ The Virgin Suicides (1999)   *- Sofia Coppola*
- ☐ Boys Don't Cry (1999)   *- Kimberly Peirce*
- ☐ American Psycho (2000)   *- Mary Harron*
- ☐ Monsoon Wedding (2001)   *- Mira Nair*
- ☐ Real Women Have Curves (2002)   *- Patricia Cardoso*
- ☐ Bend It Like Beckham (2003)   *- Gurinder Chadha*
- ☐ Something's Gotta Give (2003)   *- Nancy Meyers*
- ☐ Monster (2003)   *- Patty Jenkins*
- ☐ Whale Rider (2003)   *- Niki Caro*
- ☐ Thirteen (2003)   *- Catherine Hardwick*
- ☐ Persepolis (2007)   *- Marjane Satrapi*
- ☐ Fish Tank (2009)   *- Andrea Arnold*
- ☐ Winter's Bone (2010)   *- Debra Granik*
- ☐ We Need to Talk About Kevin (2011)   *- Lynne Ramsay*
- ☐ Stories We Tell (2012)   *- Sarah Polley*
- ☐ Frozen (2013)   *- Jennifer Lee & Chris Buck*
- ☐ The Babadook (2014)   *- Jennifer Kent*
- ☐ Selma (2014)   *- Ava DuVernay*
- ☐ Hustlers (2019)   *- Lorene Scafaria*
- ☐ The Farewell (2019)   *- Lulu Wang*
- ☐ Little Women (2019)   *- Greta Gerwig*
- ☐ Portrait of a Lady on Fire (2019)   *- Celine Sciamma*
- ☐ Nomadland (2020)   *- Chloé Zhao*
- ☐ First Cow (2020)   *- Kelly Reichardt*
- ☐ Promising Young Woman (2020)   *- Emerald Fennell*

An Odd Couple

A wildly popular movie trope is the mismatched duo, it spans all genres and age ranges. Watch a movie featuring an odd couple to complete this challenge.

Movie Watched:

_____

Directed By: Year Released:

_____   _____

Starring: Date Completed:

_____   _____

Your Review

_____

_____

_____

_____   ☆ ☆ ☆ ☆ ☆

Would you recommend it, and if so to who?

_____

_____

How could the duo be even more mismatched?

_____

_____

Some excellent odd couple movies are listed below. For other suggestions look for "odd couple movies" or "buddy cop/comedy movies" online. Also, don't forget to ask friends for their thoughts!

- ☐ Sons of the Desert (1933)
- ☐ Heaven Knows, Mr. Allison (1957)
- ☐ The Defiant Ones (1958)
- ☐ Il Sorpasso (1962)
- ☐ The Fortune Cookie (1966)
- ☐ In the Heat of the Night (1967)
- ☐ The Odd Couple (1968)
- ☐ Red Sun (1971)
- ☐ Harold and Maude (1971)
- ☐ The Front Page (1974)
- ☐ Blazing Saddles (1974)
- ☐ Silver Streak (1976)
- ☐ The In-Laws (1979)
- ☐ Stir Crazy (1980)
- ☐ Any Which Way You Can (1980)
- ☐ My Favorite Year (1982)
- ☐ 48 Hrs. (1982)
- ☐ Volunteers (1985)
- ☐ Back to School (1986)
- ☐ Crossroads (1986)
- ☐ Dragnet (1987)
- ☐ Planes, Trains & Automobiles (1987)
- ☐ Lethal Weapon (1987)
- ☐ Twins (1988)
- ☐ Midnight Run (1988)
- ☐ Big Business (1988)
- ☐ Red Heat (1988)
- ☐ See No Evil, Hear No Evil (1989)
- ☐ Guarding Tess (1994)
- ☐ Driving Miss Daisy (1989)
- ☐ Turner & Hooch (1989)
- ☐ Point Break (1991)
- ☐ Grumpy Old Men (1993)
- ☐ Muriel's Wedding (1994)
- ☐ Die Hard with a Vengeance (1995)
- ☐ Toy Story (1995)
- ☐ Bulletproof (1996)
- ☐ Men in Black (1997)
- ☐ Nothing to Lose (1997)
- ☐ Taxi (1998, 2004)
- ☐ Rush Hour (1998)
- ☐ Lawn Dogs (1998)
- ☐ Flawless (1999)
- ☐ Notting Hill (1999)
- ☐ Romeo Must Die (2000)
- ☐ Lilo & Stitch (2002)
- ☐ Anger Management (2003)
- ☐ The Matador (2005)
- ☐ Ratatouille (2007)
- ☐ Live Free or Die Hard (2007)
- ☐ From Paris with Love (2010)
- ☐ The Intouchables (2011)
- ☐ Gone Girl (2014)
- ☐ Central Intelligence (2016)
- ☐ The Nice Guys (2016)
- ☐ Bright (2017)
- ☐ The Disaster Artist (2017)
- ☐ The Lighthouse (2019)
- ☐ The Peanut Butter Falcon (2019)

The 1990s

In October 1994 cinemagoers had a tough decision: Pulp Fiction, Shawshank Redemption, Lion King or Jurassic Park? Your tough decision is to pick a 90s movie for this challenge.

Movie Watched:

_____

Directed By: Year Released:

_____   _____

Starring: Date Completed:

_____   _____

Your Review

_____

_____

_____

_____   ☆ ☆ ☆ ☆ ☆

Would you recommend it, and if so to who?

_____

_____

Pulp Fiction, Shawshank, Lion King or Jurassic Park?

_____

_____

We're sure you can find 100s of examples of 1990s movies to watch, for this list below we've focused on some of the more underrated/underseen movies. If what you watch was released in the 90s, you've completed the challenge.

- ☐ Darkman (1990)
- ☐ Joe Vs the Volcano (1990)
- ☐ Miller's Crossing (1990)
- ☐ Mo' Better Blues (1990)
- ☐ Pump Up the Volume (1990)
- ☐ Q&A (1990)
- ☐ To Sleep with Anger (1990)
- ☐ Tremors (1990)
- ☐ Trust (1990)
- ☐ LA Story (1991)
- ☐ Toy Soldiers (1991)
- ☐ Chaplin (1992)
- ☐ Jamón, Jamón (1992)
- ☐ One False Move (1992)
- ☐ Twin Peaks: Fire Walk with Me (1992)
- ☐ Benny and Joon (1993)
- ☐ Matinee (1993)
- ☐ Red Rock West (1993)
- ☐ Six Degrees of Separation (1993)
- ☐ Swimming With Sharks (1994)
- ☐ Clockers (1995)
- ☐ Devil In a Blue Dress (1995)
- ☐ Strange Days (1995)
- ☐ Waterworld (1995)
- ☐ Albino Alligator (1996)
- ☐ Beautiful Girls (1996)
- ☐ The Cable Guy (1996)
- ☐ Feeling Minnesota (1996)
- ☐ Freeway (1996)
- ☐ Night Falls on Manhattan (1996)
- ☐ That Thing You Do! (1996)
- ☐ A Very Brady Sequel (1996)
- ☐ The Game (1997)
- ☐ Gattaca (1997)
- ☐ Jackie Brown (1997)
- ☐ One Eight Seven (1997)
- ☐ In the Company of Men (1997)
- ☐ Seven Years in Tibet (1997)
- ☐ The Spanish Prisoner (1997)
- ☐ Can't Hardly Wait (1998)
- ☐ Dark City (1998)
- ☐ Happiness (1998)
- ☐ Small Soldiers (1998)
- ☐ A Simple Plan (1998)
- ☐ Velvet Goldmine (1998)
- ☐ Very Bad Things (1998)
- ☐ Zero Effect (1998)
- ☐ Election (1999)
- ☐ Eyes Wide Shut (1999)
- ☐ Ghost Dog: The Way of The Samurai (1999)
- ☐ Go (1999)
- ☐ Idle Hands (1999)
- ☐ Office Space (1999)
- ☐ Ravenous (1999)
- ☐ Stir Of Echoes (1999)
- ☐ Ten Things I Hate About You (1999)
- ☐ Two Hands (1999)

Best Picture Winner

The Academy Awards are seen as the industry's go-to award show, with Best Picture the most prestigious of all prizes. Watch a winner of the Best Picture award.

Movie Watched:

_____

Directed By: Year Released:

_____   _____

Starring: Date Completed:

_____   _____

Your Review

_____

_____

_____

_____   ☆ ☆ ☆ ☆ ☆

Would you recommend it, and if so to who?

_____

_____

Of the Best Picture winners you've seen, which is the best?

_____

_____

There are too many Best Picture winners to list on this page, and the list is easily discoverable online. Feel free to expand this challenge to include the top award from other notable film celebrations e.g.

- The Academy Award's Best Picture Winner
- Cannes Film Festival's Palme d'Or
- BAFTA's Best Film
- The Golden Globes Best Motion Picture – Drama, Musical or Comedy, Foreign Language or Animated
- Independent Spirit Awards Best Feature Film
- MTV Awards Best Movie

If you dare, you could even watch a Worst Picture award from the Golden Raspberry's (Razzies)!

Use the space below to compile your own watchlist to complete this challenge.

- ☐
- ☐
- ☐
- ☐
- ☐
- ☐
- ☐
- ☐
- ☐
- ☐

Animated

Animated movies aren't just for children. Most targeted at children have "grown-up" jokes hidden in plain sight. Watch an animated movie to complete this challenge.

Movie Watched:

_____

Directed By: Year Released:

_____   _____

Starring: Date Completed:

_____   _____

Your Review

_____

_____

_____

_____   ☆ ☆ ☆ ☆ ☆

Would you recommend it, and if so to who?

_____

_____

Which movie would you like to see an animated remake of?

_____

_____

Any animated movie can be watched for this challenge including a Japanese Anime movie. Our recommendations list below is mainly focused on more grown-up animation.

- ☐ Yellow Submarine (1968)
- ☐ Fritz the Cat (1972)
- ☐ Fantastic Planet (1973)
- ☐ Watership Down (1978)
- ☐ American Pop (1981)
- ☐ Heavy Metal (1981)
- ☐ Son of the White Mare (1981)
- ☐ The Last Unicorn (1982)
- ☐ The Secret of NIMH (1982)
- ☐ Fire and Ice (1983)
- ☐ Angel's Egg (1985)
- ☐ Akira (1988)
- ☐ Bebe's Kids (1992)
- ☐ The Nightmare Before Christmas (1993)
- ☐ Ghost in the Shell (1995)
- ☐ Beavis and Butt-Head Do America (1996)
- ☐ Perfect Blue (1997)
- ☐ Todd McFarlane's Spawn (1997)
- ☐ Princess Mononoke (1997)
- ☐ The Iron Giant (1999)
- ☐ South Park: Bigger, Longer & Uncut (1999)
- ☐ Spirited Away (2001)
- ☐ Cowboy Bebop: The Movie (2001)
- ☐ The Triplets of Belleville (2003)
- ☐ A Scanner Darkly (2006)
- ☐ Paprika (2006)
- ☐ Persepolis (2007)
- ☐ Waltz with Bashir (2008)
- ☐ Mary and Max (2009)
- ☐ Fantastic Mr. Fox (2009)
- ☐ 9 (2009)
- ☐ The Wind Rises (2013)
- ☐ Anomalisa (2015)
- ☐ Your Name (2016)
- ☐ Sausage Party (2016)

A Feature-Length Documentary

Feature-length documentaries often receive theatrical releases and tell stories with as much drama as a traditional movie. Pick one to watch for this challenge.

Movie Watched:

_____

Directed By: Year Released:

_____   _____

Starring: Date Completed:

_____   _____

Your Review

_____

_____

_____

_____

_____ ☆ ☆ ☆ ☆ ☆

Would you recommend it, and if so to who?

_____

_____

If there was a movie adaptation, who would you cast?

_____

_____

These are just a few that captured our imagination. Search for a documentary on a topic that interests you.

- ☐ Woodstock (1970)
- ☐ Pumping Iron (1977)
- ☐ A Brief History of Time (1991)
- ☐ Hoop Dreams (1994)
- ☐ When We Were Kings (1996)
- ☐ Hands on a Hardbody: The Documentary (1997)
- ☐ American Movie (1999)
- ☐ Bowling for Columbine (2002)
- ☐ Biggie & Tupac (2002)
- ☐ Touching the Void (2003)
- ☐ Capturing the Friedmans (2003)
- ☐ Fahrenheit 9/11 (2004)
- ☐ Grizzly Man (2005)
- ☐ Murderball (2005)
- ☐ Jesus Camp (2006)
- ☐ An Inconvenient Truth (2006)
- ☐ The King of Kong: A Fistful of Quarters (2007)
- ☐ Dear Zachary: A Letter to a Son About His Father (2008)
- ☐ Waltz with Bashir (2008)
- ☐ Man on Wire (2008)
- ☐ Anvil! The Story of Anvil (2008)
- ☐ Senna (2010)
- ☐ Exit Through the Gift Shop (2010)
- ☐ 20 Feet from Stardom (2013)
- ☐ Life Itself (2014)
- ☐ Electric Boogaloo: The Wild, Untold Story of Cannon Films (2014)
- ☐ Lady, You Shot Me: The Life and Death of Sam Cooke (2014)
- ☐ Amy (2015)
- ☐ Call Me Lucky (2015)
- ☐ The Death of "Superman Lives": What Happened? (2015)
- ☐ I Am Not Your Negro (2016)
- ☐ They Shall Not Grow Old (2018)
- ☐ Free Solo (2018)
- ☐ The Inventor: Out for Blood in Silicon Valley (2019)
- ☐ Crip Camp: A Disability Revolution (2020)
- ☐ My Octopus Teacher (2020)

A Current or Previous Crush

We know you've watched a movie, an actor/actress comes on the screen, and you're compelled to see more of them. Here's your chance to watch one without judgement.

Movie Watched:

_____

Directed By: Year Released:

_____   _____

Starring: Date Completed:

_____   _____

Your Review

_____

_____

_____

_____   ☆ ☆ ☆ ☆ ☆

Would you recommend it, and if so to who?

_____

_____

Who did you choose?

_____

_____

We're not going to offer any suggestions here, as everyone has different tastes. We will however leave you some space to draw up your own checklist you can work your way through. Have fun!

- [ ]
- [ ]
- [ ]
- [ ]
- [ ]
- [ ]
- [ ]
- [ ]
- [ ]
- [ ]
- [ ]
- [ ]
- [ ]
- [ ]
- [ ]
- [ ]
- [ ]
- [ ]
- [ ]
- [ ]
- [ ]
- [ ]
- [ ]

Black and White

Watch either something originally filmed in black and white due to budget/age/aesthetic choice, or a new film that received a "Noir" re-release after its traditional theatrical run.

Movie Watched:

_____

Directed By: Year Released:

_____   _____

Starring: Date Completed:

_____   _____

Your Review

_____

_____

_____

_____

_____ ☆ ☆ ☆ ☆ ☆

Would you recommend it, and if so to who?

_____

_____

Have you seen a "Noir" or colorised re-release? If so, which?

_____

_____

We're sure you can find an old black and white movie to watch for this challenge, so here is a list of modern movies where black and white was a style choice.

- ☐ Multiple Maniacs (1970)
- ☐ Paper Moon (1973)
- ☐ Lenny (1974)
- ☐ Young Frankenstein (1974)
- ☐ Eraserhead (1977)
- ☐ Manhattan (1979)
- ☐ The Elephant Man (1980)
- ☐ Raging Bull (1980)
- ☐ Stranger Than Paradise (1984)
- ☐ Wings of Desire (1987)
- ☐ Schindler's List (1993)
- ☐ Clerks (1994)
- ☐ Ed Wood (1994)
- ☐ Following (1998)
- ☐ Pi (1998)
- ☐ The Man Who Wasn't There (2001)
- ☐ Good Night, and Good Luck (2005)
- ☐ The Artist (2011)
- ☐ Frances Ha (2012)
- ☐ Much Ado About Nothing (2012)
- ☐ Ida (2013)
- ☐ Nebraska (2013)
- ☐ Roma (2018)
- ☐ Cold War (2018)
- ☐ The Lighthouse (2019)

These movies were released in colour but received a black and white re-release for an alternate aesthetic.

- ☐ The Mist (2007)
- ☐ Mad Max: Fury Road (2015)
- ☐ Logan (2017)
- ☐ Parasite (2019)
- ☐ Zack Snyder's Justice League (2021)

English Language, Foreign Director

Many successful foreign directors are lured to Hollywood with the promise of bigger budgets and wider audiences. Watch an English movie, directed by a foreign director.

Movie Watched:

Directed By: Year Released:

Starring: Date Completed:

Your Review

☆ ☆ ☆ ☆ ☆

Would you recommend it, and if so to who?

Will you seek out the director's native language movies?

There are lots of options for this challenge. Here are some we've enjoyed. You could also look up the director of each of these for other options.

- ☐ The Young One (1960)
- ☐ Repulsion (1965)
- ☐ Blow-up (1966)
- ☐ Fahrenheit 451 (1966)
- ☐ Chinatown (1974)
- ☐ Hammett (1982)
- ☐ The NeverEnding Story (1984)
- ☐ Amadeus (1984)
- ☐ Flesh+Blood (1985)
- ☐ The Name of the Rose (1986)
- ☐ RoboCop (1987)
- ☐ Hard Target (1993)
- ☐ Leon (1994)
- ☐ Desperado (1995)
- ☐ A Little Princess (1995)
- ☐ Sense and Sensibility (1995)
- ☐ Breaking the Waves (1996)
- ☐ Face/Off (1997)
- ☐ The Congress (2013)
- ☐ Alien Resurrection (1997)
- ☐ In the Mood for Love (2000)
- ☐ The Others (2001)
- ☐ Killing Me Softly (2002)
- ☐ Evil (2003)
- ☐ It's All About Love (2003)
- ☐ Gothika (2003)
- ☐ 21 Grams (2003)
- ☐ Dogville (2003)
- ☐ Hellboy (2004)
- ☐ Derailed (2005)
- ☐ The Constant Gardener (2005)
- ☐ Rescue Dawn (2006)
- ☐ The Lives of Others (2006)
- ☐ Children of Men (2006)
- ☐ Funny Games (2007)
- ☐ Rendition (2007)
- ☐ The Invasion (2007)
- ☐ My Blueberry Nights (2007)
- ☐ La Vie en Rose (2007)
- ☐ Antichrist (2009)
- ☐ The Girl with the Dragon Tattoo (2009)
- ☐ District 9 (2009)
- ☐ The Tourist (2010)
- ☐ Drive (2011)
- ☐ Tinker Tailor Soldier Spy (2011)
- ☐ Cloud Atlas (2012)
- ☐ The Congress (2013)
- ☐ Prisoners (2013)
- ☐ The Impossible (2013)
- ☐ The Last Stand (2013)
- ☐ Snowpiercer (2013)
- ☐ Stoker (2013)
- ☐ Dead Man Down (2013)
- ☐ Grace of Monaco (2014)
- ☐ Birdman (2014)
- ☐ RoboCop (2014)
- ☐ Youth (2015)
- ☐ The Lobster (2015)

Place Name in the Title

Watch a movie with a place name in the title. The place can be real (Gangs of New York), fictional (The Labyrinth), or alluded (The Place Beyond the Pines).

Movie Watched:

_____

Directed By: Year Released:

_____   _____

Starring: Date Completed:

_____   _____

Your Review

_____

_____

_____

_____

_____   ☆ ☆ ☆ ☆ ☆

Would you recommend it, and if so to who?

_____

_____

Was it a place you've been to, or would like to visit?

_____

_____

Listed below is a small selection to get you started. How many have you seen?

- [ ] Casablanca (1942)
- [ ] Five Graves to Cairo (1943)
- [ ] Sunset Boulevard (1950)
- [ ] The Killer That Stalked New York (1950)
- [ ] Judgment at Nuremberg (1961)
- [ ] Funeral in Berlin (1966)
- [ ] The Boston Strangler (1968)
- [ ] The Texas Chainsaw Massacre (1974)
- [ ] The Amityville Horror (1979)
- [ ] Escape From New York (1981)
- [ ] Moscow on the Hudson (1984)
- [ ] Down and Out in Beverly Hills (1986)
- [ ] Mississippi Burning (1988)
- [ ] Last Exit to Brooklyn (1989)
- [ ] Philadelphia (1993)
- [ ] Sleepless in Seattle (1993)
- [ ] The Bridges of Madison County (1995)
- [ ] Rumble in the Bronx (1995)
- [ ] Fargo (1996)
- [ ] Fear and Loathing in Las Vegas (1998)
- [ ] Mulholland Drive (2001)
- [ ] Orange County (2002)
- [ ] Wimbledon (2004)
- [ ] Hollywoodland (2006)
- [ ] Paris, Je T'aime (2006)
- [ ] In Bruges (2008)
- [ ] Midnight In Paris (2011)
- [ ] Dallas Buyers Club (2013)
- [ ] Sunshine on Leith (2013)
- [ ] The Grand Budapest Hotel (2014)
- [ ] Straight Outta Compton (2015)
- [ ] The Stanford Prison Experiment (2015)
- [ ] The Florida Project (2017)
- [ ] Three Billboards Outside Ebbing, Missouri (2017)
- [ ] If Beale Street Could Talk (2018)
- [ ] The Trial of the Chicago 7 (2020)

Based on Comic/Graphic Novel

Despite Marvel and DC controlling the box office recently, it doesn't mean all graphic novels feature superheroes. Watch one to complete this challenge (or watch more superheroes).

Movie Watched:

_____

Directed By: Year Released:

_____   _____

Starring: Date Completed:

_____   _____

Your Review

_____

_____

_____

_____   ☆ ☆ ☆ ☆ ☆

Would you recommend it, and if so to who?

_____

_____

Which did you watch, a superhero movie or not?

_____

_____

You can of course watch more superhero movies to complete this challenge, but if that's not your bag we've got a little list we prepared.

- ☐ Dick Tracy (1990)
- ☐ Riki-Oh: The Story of Ricky (1991)
- ☐ The Crow (1994)
- ☐ Tank Girl (1995)
- ☐ Crying Freeman (1995)
- ☐ Judge Dredd (1995)
- ☐ Men in Black (1997)
- ☐ Blade (1998)
- ☐ Virus (1999)
- ☐ From Hell (2001)
- ☐ Blade II (2002)
- ☐ Men in Black II (2002)
- ☐ Road to Perdition (2002)
- ☐ Oldboy (2003)
- ☐ Blade: Trinity (2004)
- ☐ AVP: Alien vs. Predator (2004)
- ☐ The Wedding Party (2005)
- ☐ Constantine (2005)
- ☐ Sin City (2005)
- ☐ A History of Violence (2005)
- ☐ V for Vendetta (2005)
- ☐ 300 (2006)
- ☐ Aliens vs Predator: Requiem (2007)
- ☐ Wanted (2008)
- ☐ The Spirit (2008)
- ☐ Punisher: War Zone (2008)
- ☐ Surrogates (2009)
- ☐ The Losers (2010)
- ☐ Scott Pilgrim vs. the World (2010)
- ☐ RED (2010)
- ☐ Cowboys & Aliens (2011)
- ☐ Dredd (2012)
- ☐ Men in Black 3 (2012)
- ☐ 2 Guns (2013)
- ☐ Oblivion (2013)
- ☐ Snowpiercer (2013)
- ☐ RED 2 (2013)
- ☐ 13 Sins (2014)
- ☐ Kingsman: The Secret Service (2014)
- ☐ Sin City: A Dame to Kill For (2014)
- ☐ Edge of Tomorrow (2014)
- ☐ 300: Rise of an Empire (2014)
- ☐ Valerian and the City of a Thousand Planets (2017)
- ☐ Ghost in the Shell (2017)
- ☐ Atomic Blonde (2017)
- ☐ Kingsman: The Golden Circle (2017)
- ☐ The Death of Stalin (2017)
- ☐ Alita: Battle Angel (2019)
- ☐ Extraction (2020)
- ☐ The Kitchen (2019)
- ☐ Polar (2019)

Starring Blood Relatives

"We were like one big family" you often hear in interviews promoting a movie. Well, this challenge is to watch a movie that stars actual family members.

Movie Watched:

_____

Directed By: Year Released:

_____   _____

Starring: Date Completed:

_____   _____

Your Review

_____

_____

_____

_____   ☆ ☆ ☆ ☆ ☆

Would you recommend it, and if so to who?

_____

_____

Which actors were related and how?

_____

_____

Here are just a few examples of relatives working together.

- ☐ Duck Soup (1933)
  - *Chico, Harpo, Groucho, Gummo, and Zeppo Marx (Siblings)*
- ☐ Cast a Giant Shadow (1966)
  - *Kirk Douglas and Michael Douglas (Father and Son)*
- ☐ Silent Night, Lonely Night (1969)
  - *Lloyd Bridges and Jeff Bridges (Father and Son)*
- ☐ Paper Moon (1973)
  - *Ryan O'Neal and Tatum O'Neal (Father Daughter)*
- ☐ Alice Doesn't Live Here Anymore (1974)
  - *Diane Ladd and Laura Dern (Mother and Daughter)*
- ☐ Caddyshack (1980)
  - *Bill Murray & Brian Doyle-Murray (Siblings)*
- ☐ Roar (1981)
  - *Tippi Hedren and Melanie Griffith (Mother and Daughter)*
- ☐ Rumble Fish (1983)
  - *Nicolas Cage and Sofia Coppola (Cousins)*
- ☐ Wall Street (1987)
  - *Martin Sheen and Charlie Sheen (Father and Son)*
- ☐ The Fabulous Baker Boys (1989)
  - *Jeff Bridges and Beau Bridges (Siblings)*
- ☐ Calvary (2014)
  - *Brendan Gleeson and Domhnall Gleeson (Father and Son)*
- ☐ Good Will Hunting (1997)
  - *Ben Affleck and Casey Affleck (Siblings)*
- ☐ The Royal Tenenbaums (2001)
  - *Owen Wilson and Luke Wilson (Siblings)*
- ☐ Donnie Darko (2001)
  - *Jake Gyllenhaal and Maggie Gyllenhaal (Siblings)*
- ☐ Lara Croft: Tomb Raider (2001)
  - *Jon Voight and Angelina Jolie (Father and Daughter)*
- ☐ Zoolander (2001)
  - *Jerry Stiller and Ben Stiller (Father and Son)*
- ☐ The Pursuit of Happyness (2006)
  - *Will Smith and Jaden Smith (Father and Son)*
- ☐ Melancholia (2011)
  - *Stellan Skarsgård and Alexander Skarsgård (Father and Son)*
- ☐ The Disaster Artist
  - *James Franco and Dave Franco (Siblings)*

A Musical

Musicals were once a staple of Hollywood, but thanks to Les Misérables and The World's Greatest Showman they're back with a bang. Singing along is allowed for this challenge.

Movie Watched:

_____

Directed By: Year Released:

_____   _____

Starring: Date Completed:

_____   _____

Your Review

_____

_____

_____

_____

_____   ☆ ☆ ☆ ☆ ☆

Would you recommend it, and if so to who?

_____

_____

Which was the best song?

_____

_____

We know musicals aren't everyone's cup of tea, that's why we've put together this list of non-traditional musicals for you.

- ☐ Fantasia (1940)
- ☐ Dumbo (1941)
- ☐ A Star Is Born (1954)
- ☐ Mary Poppins (1964)
- ☐ My Fair Lady (1964)
- ☐ Chitty Chitty Bang Bang (1968)
- ☐ The Rocky Horror Picture Show (1975)
- ☐ Grease (1978)
- ☐ The Wiz (1978)
- ☐ Hair (1979)
- ☐ 9 to 5 (1980)
- ☐ The Blues Brothers (1980)
- ☐ Pink Floyd: The Wall (1982)
- ☐ Purple Rain (1984)
- ☐ Little Shop of Horrors (1986)
- ☐ Labyrinth (1986)
- ☐ Cry-Baby (1990)
- ☐ Aladdin (1992)
- ☐ South Park: Bigger, Longer and Uncut (1999)
- ☐ Dancer in the Dark (2000)
- ☐ Hedwig and the Angry Inch (2001)
- ☐ Happiness of the Katakuris (2001)
- ☐ Moulin Rouge! (2001)
- ☐ Chicago (2002)
- ☐ The Producers (2005)
- ☐ Dreamgirls (2006)
- ☐ Hairspray (2007)
- ☐ Sweeney Todd: The Demon Barber of Fleet Street (2007)
- ☐ Mamma Mia! (2008)
- ☐ Repo! The Genetic Opera (2008)
- ☐ Rock of Ages (2012)
- ☐ Les Misérables (2012)
- ☐ The Greatest Showman (2017)
- ☐ Cats (2019)

Creature Feature

The exact opposite of a musical and one of the greatest terms that describes an entire subgenre. Watch either a classic or modern monster movie, to complete this challenge.

Movie Watched:

_____

Directed By: Year Released:

_____   _____

Starring: Date Completed:

_____   _____

Your Review

_____

_____

_____

_____

_____   ☆ ☆ ☆ ☆ ☆

Would you recommend it, and if so to who?

_____

_____

What do you consider to be the best monster movie?

_____

_____

A mixture of classic and modern monster movies for you to gain some inspiration from.

- ☐ Frankenstein (1931)
- ☐ Werewolf of London (1935)
- ☐ The Wolf Man (1941)
- ☐ Creature from the Black Lagoon (1954)
- ☐ The Curse of the Werewolf (1961)
- ☐ Island of Terror (1966)
- ☐ Jaws (1975)
- ☐ Alien (1979)
- ☐ An American Werewolf in London (1981)
- ☐ Swamp Thing (1982)
- ☐ Gremlins (1984)
- ☐ The Fly (1986)
- ☐ Little Shop of Horrors (1986)
- ☐ The Monster Squad (1987)
- ☐ Anaconda (1997)
- ☐ Ginger Snaps (2000)
- ☐ Van Helsing (2004)
- ☐ Rogue (2007)
- ☐ Warbirds (2008)
- ☐ Hydra (2009)
- ☐ Malibu Shark Attack (2009)
- ☐ Piranha 3D (2010)
- ☐ Sharktopus (2010)
- ☐ The Wolfman (2010)
- ☐ The Cabin in the Woods (2011)
- ☐ Frankenweenie (2012)
- ☐ Age of Dinosaurs (2013)
- ☐ Sharknado (2013)
- ☐ Pacific Rim (2013)
- ☐ Werewolf Rising (2014)
- ☐ Godzilla (2014)
- ☐ Goosebumps (2015)
- ☐ The Shallows (2016)
- ☐ It (2017)
- ☐ Rampage (2018)
- ☐ The Meg (2018)

Foreign Movie

"Once you overcome the 1-inch-tall barrier of subtitles, you will be introduced to so many more amazing films" - Bong Joon-ho.
He was right, so what are you watching for this challenge?

Movie Watched:

_____

Directed By: Year Released:

_____   _____

Starring: Date Completed:

_____   _____

Your Review

_____

_____

_____

_____   ☆ ☆ ☆ ☆ ☆

Would you recommend it, and if so to who?

_____

_____

Do you watch subtitled movies? Which are your favourites?

_____

_____

If you're familiar with foreign movies, then you probably don't need any suggestions. Otherwise, consider this a list of foreign movies for people who don't like foreign movies.

- ☐ M (1931)
- ☐ The Bicycle Thieves (1948)
- ☐ Seven Samurai (1954)
- ☐ Diabolique (1955)
- ☐ Yojimbo (1961)
- ☐ Das Boot (1981)
- ☐ Cinema Paradiso (1988)
- ☐ La Haine (1995)
- ☐ Life Is Beautiful (1997)
- ☐ Amores Perros (2000)
- ☐ Battle Royale (2000)
- ☐ Amélie (2001)
- ☐ Crouching Tiger, Hidden Dragon (2000)
- ☐ Spirited Away (2001)
- ☐ Y Tu Mamá También (2001)
- ☐ City of God (2002)
- ☐ Ong-Bak (2003)
- ☐ Oldboy (2003)
- ☐ Taxi (2004)
- ☐ Pan's Labyrinth (2006)
- ☐ The Lives of Others (2006)
- ☐ The Orphange (2007)
- ☐ Let the Right One In (2008)
- ☐ The Raid (2011)
- ☐ Intouchables (2011)
- ☐ A Separation (2011)
- ☐ The Hunt (2012)
- ☐ The Tribe (2014)
- ☐ Baahubali (2015)
- ☐ Train to Busan (2016)
- ☐ Parasite (2019)
- ☐ The Farewell (2019)
- ☐ Another Round (2020)

Set on a Vehicle

There is something about a movie primarily set on a vehicle that adds a little extra suspense into the proceedings. Choose one for this challenge.

Movie Watched:

_____

Directed By: Year Released:

_____   _____

Starring: Date Completed:

_____   _____

Your Review

_____

_____

_____

_____

_____   ☆ ☆ ☆ ☆ ☆

Would you recommend it, and if so to who?

_____

_____

Which vehicle was it set on? Would you choose differently?

_____

_____

These movies are all set in the future. You can find more by searching "movies set in the future" on the internet.

Planes

- ☐ Airport (1970)
- ☐ Airplane! (1980)
- ☐ Passenger 57 (1992)
- ☐ Con Air (1997)
- ☐ Air Force One (1997)
- ☐ Red Eye (2005)
- ☐ Flightplan (2005)
- ☐ Snakes on a Plane (2006)
- ☐ Flight (2012)
- ☐ Sully (2016)

Trains

- ☐ Strangers on a Train (1951)
- ☐ Von Ryan's Express (1965)
- ☐ The Taking of Pelham 123 (1974)
- ☐ Runaway Train (1985)
- ☐ Under Siege 2 (1995)
- ☐ The Polar Express (2004)
- ☐ The Darjeeling Limited (2007)
- ☐ Transsiberian (2008)
- ☐ Unstoppable (2010)
- ☐ Murder on the Orient Express (2017)

Automobiles

- ☐ The Italian Job (1969)
- ☐ Duel (1971)
- ☐ The Car (1977)
- ☐ Gone in 60 Seconds (2000)
- ☐ Collateral (2004)
- ☐ Death Proof (2007)
- ☐ Speed Racer (2008)
- ☐ Drive (2011)
- ☐ Mad Max: Fury Road (2015)
- ☐ Ford v Ferrari (2019)

Others

- ☐ The Poseidon Adventure (1972)
- ☐ Das Boot (1981)
- ☐ Blue Thunder (1983)
- ☐ Rad (1986)
- ☐ The Hunt for Red October (1990)
- ☐ Apollo 13 (1995)
- ☐ Captain Phillips (2009)
- ☐ Premium Rush (2012)
- ☐ Passengers (2016)
- ☐ The Aeronauts (2019)

When I grow up, I want to be...

What's more fun than picking apart movie depictions of your job? To complete this challenge, watch a movie that features your job, previous job, or a job you wish you had.

Movie Watched:

_____

Directed By: Year Released:

_____   _____

Starring: Date Completed:

_____   _____

Your Review

_____

_____

_____

_____   ☆ ☆ ☆ ☆ ☆

Would you recommend it, and if so to who?

_____

_____

Which job did you choose?

_____

_____

For this challenge you've got 3 options:

Your current job
This can be as loose as it needs to be, or you want it to be. E.g., if you work with computers in any form, you could watch a hacking film. If you work in medicine anything featuring doctors/hospitals etc.

Your previous job
Same as before, as loose as you want. This is more for those of you who have changed careers or retired.

A Job you wish you had
You can have as much fun with this as you want. Did you want to run a dinosaur park? Hunt vampires? Travel to space? Work with children? The only limit is your imagination.

Use the space below to compile your own watchlist to complete this challenge.

☐

☐

☐

☐

☐

☐

☐

☐

☐

The Title Contains a Number

There's just one caveat to this challenge of watching a movie that has a title containing a number: No sequels allowed! That's too easy. The number can be numeric or written.

Movie Watched:

_____

Directed By: Year Released:

_____   _____

Starring: Date Completed:

_____   _____

Your Review

_____

_____

_____

_____

_____   ☆ ☆ ☆ ☆ ☆

Would you recommend it, and if so to who?

_____

_____

_____

What was the number in the title a reference to?

_____

_____

Lots of options for this challenge. Choose one of these or see if there are any already on your watchlist.

- ☐ 42nd Street (1933)
- ☐ Seven Samurai (1954)
- ☐ The Seventh Seal (1957)
- ☐ 12 Angry Men (1957)
- ☐ Plan 9 from Outer Space (1957)
- ☐ The 400 Blows (1959)
- ☐ 13 Ghosts (1960)
- ☐ Ocean's Eleven (1960)
- ☐ 101 Dalmatians (1961)
- ☐ 2001: A Space Odyssey (1968)
- ☐ Five Easy Pieces (1970)
- ☐ The Cat o' Nine Tails (1971)
- ☐ Phase IV (1974)
- ☐ 10 (1979)
- ☐ Friday the 13th (1980)
- ☐ Ms .45 (1981)
- ☐ Class of 1984 (1982)
- ☐ Four Rooms (1995)
- ☐ Twelve Monkeys (1995)
- ☐ Apollo 13 (1995)
- ☐ Nine Months (1995)
- ☐ Se7en (1995)
- ☐ The Fifth Element (1997)
- ☐ Lock, Stock and Two Smoking Barrels (1998)
- ☐ The Sixth Sense (1999)
- ☐ U-571 (2000)
- ☐ 28 Days Later (2002)
- ☐ Eight Legged Freaks (2002)
- ☐ One Missed Call (2003)
- ☐ A Tale of Two Sisters (2003)
- ☐ House of 1000 Corpses (2003)
- ☐ 13 Going on 30 (2004)
- ☐ Fantastic Four (2005)
- ☐ 300 (2006)
- ☐ 1408 (2007)
- ☐ 30 Days of Night (2007)
- ☐ P2 (2007)
- ☐ 10,000 BC (2008)
- ☐ Four Christmases (2008)
- ☐ 2012 (2009)
- ☐ 17 Again (2009)
- ☐ District 9 (2009)
- ☐ 3 Idiots (2009)
- ☐ 9 (2009)
- ☐ (500) Days of Summer (2009)
- ☐ 13 Assassins (2010)
- ☐ Four Lions (2010)
- ☐ Apollo 18 (2011)
- ☐ 50/50 (2011)
- ☐ Zero Dark Thirty (2012)
- ☐ 21 Jump Street (2012)
- ☐ 2 Guns (2013)
- ☐ 12 Years a Slave (2013)
- ☐ The Hateful Eight (2015)
- ☐ 31 (2016)
- ☐ The 5th Wave (2016)
- ☐ 47 Meters Down (2017)
- ☐ 1922 (2017)
- ☐ mid90s (2018)
- ☐ First Man (2018)
- ☐ 7 Days in Entebbe (2018)
- ☐ Eighth Grade (2018)
- ☐ Ready Player One (2018)
- ☐ 1917 (2019)
- ☐ Plus One (2019)
- ☐ The Trial of the Chicago 7 (2020)

An Epic

To complete this challenge, we want you to watch an epic movie. Something long, large scale, a spectacle to behold. Either traditional or something more modern.

Movie Watched:

_____

Directed By: Year Released:

_____   _____

Starring: Date Completed:

_____   _____

Your Review

_____

_____

_____

_____   ☆ ☆ ☆ ☆ ☆

Would you recommend it, and if so to who?

_____

_____

_____

Do you prefer traditional epics, or more modern ones?

_____

_____

Modern epics are different to classic epics, but both tell big stories in bold ways. Epic movies haven't gone, they're just different nowadays.

- ☐ Gone With the Wind (1939)
- ☐ Quo Vadis (1951)
- ☐ Seven Samurai (1954)
- ☐ The Ten Commandments (1956)
- ☐ The Bridge on the River Kwai (1957)
- ☐ Ben-Hur (1959)
- ☐ Spartacus (1960)
- ☐ Lawrence of Arabia (1962)
- ☐ Cleopatra (1963)
- ☐ Doctor Zhivago (1965)
- ☐ War and Peace (1966)
- ☐ The Good, the Bad, and the Ugly (1966)
- ☐ 2001: A Space Odyssey (1968)
- ☐ Once Upon a Time in the West (1968)
- ☐ The Godfather (1972)
- ☐ Apocalypse Now (1979)
- ☐ Gandhi (1982)
- ☐ Fitzcarraldo (1982)
- ☐ Amadeus (1984)
- ☐ Once Upon a Time in America (1984)
- ☐ Ran (1985)
- ☐ The Last Emperor (1987)
- ☐ The English Patient (1996)
- ☐ Titanic (1997)
- ☐ Gladiator (2000)
- ☐ Crouching Tiger, Hidden Dragon (2000)
- ☐ The Lord of the Rings trilogy (2001-2003)
- ☐ Master and Commander (2003)
- ☐ King Kong (2005)
- ☐ 300 (2006)
- ☐ There Will Be Blood (2007)
- ☐ Avatar (2009)
- ☐ Mulan (2020)

A Silent Movie

Many people nowadays will turn subtitles on for movies, so they don't miss what is being said. At the dawn of cinema, viewers didn't have the option. Watch a silent movie.

Movie Watched:

_____

Directed By: Year Released:

_____   _____

Starring: Date Completed:

_____   _____

Your Review

_____

_____

_____

_____   ☆ ☆ ☆ ☆ ☆

Would you recommend it, and if so to who?

_____

_____

Have you seen many silent movies; will you seek out more?

_____

_____

By the early 1930s, the era of silent film was pretty much over. So most pre-1930's will be silent movies. Here are some suggestions, along with some more recent options.

- ☐ The Cabinet of Dr. Caligari (1920)
- ☐ The Phantom Carriage (1921)
- ☐ The Kid (1921)
- ☐ Nosferatu (1922)
- ☐ Cœur fidèle (1923)
- ☐ The Thief of Bagdad (1924)
- ☐ Sherlock, Jr. (1924)
- ☐ He Who Gets Slapped (1924)
- ☐ Greed (1924)
- ☐ The Last Laugh (1924)
- ☐ The Gold Rush (1925)
- ☐ Battleship Potemkin (1925)
- ☐ A Page of Madness (1926)
- ☐ Faust (1926)
- ☐ The General (1926)
- ☐ Metropolis (1927)
- ☐ Sunrise: A Song of Two Humans (1927)
- ☐ The Circus (1928)
- ☐ The Passion of Joan of Arc (1928)
- ☐ The Wind (1928)
- ☐ The Fall of the House of Usher (1928)
- ☐ Man with a Movie Camera (1929)
- ☐ Pandora's Box (1929)
- ☐ Diary of a Lost Girl (1929)
- ☐ Earth (1930)
- ☐ City Lights (1931)
- ☐ Limite (1931)
- ☐ Modern Times (1936)
- ☐ Le Révélateur (1968)
- ☐ Hotel Monterey (1972)
- ☐ Horizons (1973)
- ☐ Les Hautes solitudes (1974)
- ☐ Silent Movie (1976)
- ☐ At Sea (2007)
- ☐ The Artist (2011)

Crime

For this challenge, you should watch a crime film. Seeing how criminals' minds work, and how they intend to execute their plans often brings about a compelling movie.

Movie Watched:

_____

Directed By: Year Released:

_____   _____

Starring: Date Completed:

_____   _____

Your Review

_____

_____

_____

_____

_____   ☆ ☆ ☆ ☆ ☆

Would you recommend it, and if so to who?

_____

_____

What's your favourite crime film?

_____

_____

It's entirely up to how serious of a crime you want to tackle for this challenge. It could be a heist movie, one about embezzlement, murder, or a simple misdemeanour. These are some crime movies we've enjoyed over the years.

- ☐ Double Indemnity (1944)
- ☐ Dial M for Murder (1954)
- ☐ Point Blank (1967)
- ☐ In the Heat of the Night (1967)
- ☐ Get Carter (1971)
- ☐ Chinatown (1974)
- ☐ Dog Day Afternoon (1975)
- ☐ Taxi Driver (1976)
- ☐ The Untouchables (1987)
- ☐ GoodFellas (1990)
- ☐ Léon: The Professional (1994)
- ☐ Se7en (1995)
- ☐ The Usual Suspects (1995)
- ☐ Casino (1995)
- ☐ Heat (1995)
- ☐ Fargo (1996)
- ☐ Ronin (1998)
- ☐ Ocean's Eleven (2001)
- ☐ Road to Perdition (2002)
- ☐ The Italian Job (2003)
- ☐ Inside Man (2006)
- ☐ The Departed (2006)
- ☐ Before the Devil Knows You're Dead (2007)
- ☐ Public Enemies (2009)
- ☐ The Town (2010)
- ☐ I Saw the Devil (2010)
- ☐ Drive (2011)
- ☐ Prisoners (2013)
- ☐ Only God Forgives (2013)
- ☐ Don't Breathe (2016)
- ☐ Hell or High Water (2016)
- ☐ Wind River (2017)

Disaster Movie

The fine line between plausibility and fantasy is clearly what makes cinematic depictions of natural (and unnatural) disasters so compelling. Choose one for this challenge.

Movie Watched:

_____

Directed By: Year Released:

_____   _____

Starring: Date Completed:

_____   _____

Your Review

_____

_____

_____

_____   ☆ ☆ ☆ ☆ ☆

Would you recommend it, and if so to who?

_____

_____

Rate it on a scale of 1 (Very Plausible) to 10 (Pure fantasy)

_____

_____

You know the score by now. Here are some disaster movies, check the ones you've seen, watch one that you haven't.

- ☐ The Last Days of Pompeii (1908)
- ☐ The Day the Earth Stood Still (1951)
- ☐ Godzilla (1954)
- ☐ Airport (1970)
- ☐ The Poseidon Adventure (1972)
- ☐ Earthquake (1974)
- ☐ The Towering Inferno (1974)
- ☐ Night of the Comet (1984)
- ☐ Twister (1996)
- ☐ Daylight (1996)
- ☐ Dante's Peak (1997)
- ☐ Volcano (1997)
- ☐ Deep Impact (1998)
- ☐ Godzilla (1998)
- ☐ Armageddon (1998)
- ☐ The Perfect Storm (2000)
- ☐ 28 Days Later (2002)
- ☐ The Core (2003)
- ☐ The Day After Tomorrow (2004)
- ☐ War of the Worlds (2005)
- ☐ Poseidon (2006)
- ☐ World Trade Center (2006)
- ☐ Sunshine (2007)
- ☐ Cloverfield (2008)
- ☐ The Happening (2008)
- ☐ Disaster Movie (2008)
- ☐ The Day the Earth Stood Still (2008)
- ☐ Knowing (2009)
- ☐ 2012 (2009)
- ☐ Monsters (2010)
- ☐ Unstoppable (2010)
- ☐ Skyline (2010)
- ☐ Ice Quake (2010)
- ☐ Metal Tornado (2011)
- ☐ 4:44 Last Day on Earth (2011)
- ☐ Contagion (2011)
- ☐ It's a Disaster (2012)
- ☐ The Impossible (2012)
- ☐ Aftershock (2012)
- ☐ 40 Days and Nights (2012)
- ☐ 500 MPH Storm (2013)
- ☐ 100 Degrees Below Zero (2013)
- ☐ This Is the End (2013)
- ☐ World War Z (2013)
- ☐ Sharknado (2013)
- ☐ Hours (2013)
- ☐ Pompeii (2014)
- ☐ Noah (2014)
- ☐ Godzilla (2014)
- ☐ Into the Storm (2014)
- ☐ Left Behind (2014)
- ☐ Monsters: Dark Continent (2014)
- ☐ San Andreas (2015)
- ☐ The 5th Wave (2016)
- ☐ Sharknado 4: The 4th Awakens (2016)
- ☐ Deepwater Horizon (2016)
- ☐ Geostorm (2017)
- ☐ Crawl (2019)
- ☐ Greenland (2020)
- ☐ The Mitchells vs. The Machines (2021)
- ☐ Don't Look Up (2021)
- ☐ Moonfall (2022)

Released by A24

The independent distributor/producing company A24 have taken Hollywood by storm since they formed in 2012. Watch one of their releases to complete this challenge.

Movie Watched:

_____

Directed By: Year Released:

_____   _____

Starring: Date Completed:

_____   _____

Your Review

_____

_____

_____

_____

_____ ☆ ☆ ☆ ☆ ☆

Would you recommend it, and if so to who?

_____

_____

_____

Were you aware of A24's output prior to this challenge?

_____

_____

Even if you haven't heard of A24, chances are you'll have seen something they've released. Far too many to list on one page, but this list is a good starting point.

- ☐ Spring Breakers (2012)
- ☐ The Bling Ring (2013)
- ☐ The Spectacular Now (2013)
- ☐ Enemy (2013)
- ☐ Under the Skin (2013)
- ☐ Locke (2013)
- ☐ Obvious Child (2014)
- ☐ The Rover (2014)
- ☐ Life After Beth (2014)
- ☐ Tusk (2014)
- ☐ Son of a Gun (2014)
- ☐ Laggies (2014)
- ☐ A Most Violent Year (2014)
- ☐ While We're Young (2014)
- ☐ Ex Machina (2014)
- ☐ Barely Lethal (2015)
- ☐ Amy (2015)
- ☐ The End of the Tour (2015)
- ☐ Dark Places (2015)
- ☐ Mississippi Grind (2015)
- ☐ Room (2015)
- ☐ Mojave (2015)
- ☐ The Witch (2015)
- ☐ Remember (2015)
- ☐ Krisha (2015)
- ☐ Green Room (2015)
- ☐ The Adderall Diaries (2015)
- ☐ The Lobster (2015)
- ☐ Swiss Army Man (2016)
- ☐ Equals (2015)
- ☐ American Honey (2016)
- ☐ Moonlight (2016)
- ☐ Free Fire (2016)
- ☐ It Comes at Night (2017)
- ☐ A Ghost Story (2017)
- ☐ The Florida Project (2017)
- ☐ The Killing of a Sacred Deer (2017)
- ☐ Lady Bird (2017)
- ☐ The Disaster Artist (2017)
- ☐ The Last Movie Star (2017)
- ☐ Lean on Pete (2017)
- ☐ First Reformed (2017)
- ☐ Hereditary (2018)
- ☐ Woman Walks Ahead (2017)
- ☐ Eighth Grade (2018)
- ☐ Hot Summer Nights (2017)
- ☐ Never Goin' Back (2018)
- ☐ Slice (2018)
- ☐ The Children Act (2017)
- ☐ mid90s (2018)
- ☐ Outlaws (2017)
- ☐ Climax (2018)
- ☐ Gloria Bell (2018)
- ☐ Native Son (2019)
- ☐ Under the Silver Lake (2018)
- ☐ The Souvenir (2019)
- ☐ The Last Black Man in San Francisco (2019)
- ☐ Midsommar (2019)
- ☐ The Farewell (2019)
- ☐ The Lighthouse (2019)
- ☐ Waves (2019)
- ☐ Uncut Gems (2019)
- ☐ First Cow (2019)
- ☐ Saint Maud (2019)
- ☐ Minari (2020)
- ☐ Zola (2020)
- ☐ The Green Knight (2021)
- ☐ Lamb (2021)

Favourite Director

This challenge is to watch a film directed by your favourite director. If you've already seen their whole catalogue, pick a film from another director whose work you enjoy.

Movie Watched:

_____

Directed By: Year Released:

_____   _____

Starring: Date Completed:

_____   _____

Your Review

_____

_____

_____

_____   ☆ ☆ ☆ ☆ ☆

Would you recommend it, and if so to who?

_____

_____

What is the best film this director has made?

_____

_____

There are simply far too many wonderful directors out there making excellent movies for us to even consider whittling down a list for this page.

Hopefully, you have a good idea of your favourite director(s) already. If not, we suggest looking up the director of some of your favourite films. From there you can look at their filmography and see what movies they directed you recognize and love. That should help shorten your list of directors to a handful who's work you enjoy.

Use the space below to compile your own watchlist to complete this challenge.

☐

☐

☐

☐

☐

☐

☐

☐

☐

☐

☐

☐

☐

☐

☐

Non-Human Protagonist/Antagonist

Non-human characters in movies that drive the plot will add a different challenge to the movie-making process. Watch a movie with a non-human character.

Movie Watched:

_____

Directed By: Year Released:

_____   _____

Starring: Date Completed:

_____   _____

Your Review

_____

_____

_____

_____

_____   ☆ ☆ ☆ ☆ ☆

Would you recommend it, and if so to who?

_____

_____

Pick 2 non-human characters for an "X Vs Y" movie.

_____

_____

A Robot, alien, monster, animal, a robot alien monster animal? Which are you picking for this challenge? Here are a few we've enjoyed, ask friends which they enjoyed.

- ☐ Metropolis (1927)
- ☐ King Kong (1933, 2005)
- ☐ Them! (1954)
- ☐ Godzilla (1954)
- ☐ The Red Balloon (1956)
- ☐ The Seventh Seal (1957)
- ☐ The Birds (1963)
- ☐ 2001: A Space Odyssey (1968)
- ☐ Jaws (1975)
- ☐ The Car (1977)
- ☐ Close Encounters of the Third Kind (1977)
- ☐ Homeward Bound (1980)
- ☐ The Evil Dead (1981)
- ☐ Blade Runner (1982)
- ☐ The Thing (1982)
- ☐ Cujo (1983)
- ☐ Christine (1983)
- ☐ A Nightmare on Elm Street (1984)
- ☐ Starman (1984)
- ☐ Weird Science (1985)
- ☐ Teen Wolf (1985)
- ☐ Enemy Mine (1985)
- ☐ Short Circuit (1986)
- ☐ Flight of the Navigator (1986)
- ☐ Predator (1987)
- ☐ *batteries not included (1987)
- ☐ They Live (1988)
- ☐ Candyman (1992)
- ☐ Coneheads (1993)
- ☐ Species (1995)
- ☐ Babe (1995)
- ☐ Mars Attacks! (1996)
- ☐ Bicentennial Man (1999)
- ☐ The Iron Giant (1999)
- ☐ Signs (2002)
- ☐ The Host (2006)
- ☐ Pan's Labyrinth (2006)
- ☐ The Mist (2007)
- ☐ WALL·E (2008)
- ☐ Moon (2009)
- ☐ Hachi: A Dog's Tale (2009)
- ☐ District 9 (2009)
- ☐ 9 (2009)
- ☐ Jennifer's Body (2009)
- ☐ Fantastic Mr. Fox (2009)
- ☐ Rubber (2010)
- ☐ Robot (2010)
- ☐ Thor (2011)
- ☐ Super 8 (2011)
- ☐ Rise of the Planet of the Apes (2011)
- ☐ Pacific Rim (2013)
- ☐ Under the Skin (2013)
- ☐ Her (2013)
- ☐ Ender's Game (2013)
- ☐ The Babadook (2014)
- ☐ Edge of Tomorrow (2014)
- ☐ Paddington (2014)
- ☐ Ex Machina (2014)
- ☐ Chappie (2015)
- ☐ Arrival (2016)
- ☐ Okja (2017)
- ☐ The Shape of Water (2017)
- ☐ A Quiet Place (2018)
- ☐ Alita: Battle Angel (2019)
- ☐ Brightburn (2019)
- ☐ Sonic the Hedgehog (2020)
- ☐ Psycho Goreman (2020)

Show Me the Money

We're now in the realm of the billion-dollar box office. For this challenge, we want you to the movie with the biggest box office takings that you haven't already seen.

Movie Watched:

_____

Directed By: Year Released:

_____   _____

Starring: Date Completed:

_____   _____

Your Review

_____

_____

_____

_____   ☆ ☆ ☆ ☆ ☆

Would you recommend it, and if so to who?

_____

_____

Which, in your opinion, are the best big box office movies?

_____

_____

These have all made $1b at the box office (at time of writing). Search online "top lifetime grosses" for a full list.

- ☐ Avatar (2009) — $2,847,246,203
- ☐ Avengers: Endgame (2019) — $2,797,501,328
- ☐ Titanic (1997) — $2,201,647,264
- ☐ Star Wars: Episode VII - The Force Awakens (2015) — $2,069,521,700
- ☐ Avengers: Infinity War (2018) — $2,048,359,754
- ☐ Jurassic World (2015) — $1,670,516,444
- ☐ The Lion King (2019) — $1,662,899,439
- ☐ The Avengers (2012) — $1,518,815,515
- ☐ Furious 7 (2015) — $1,515,341,399
- ☐ Frozen II (2019) — $1,450,026,933
- ☐ Avengers: Age of Ultron (2015) — $1,402,809,540
- ☐ Black Panther (2018) — $1,347,597,973
- ☐ Harry Potter and the Deathly Hallows: Part 2 (2011) — $1,342,321,665
- ☐ Star Wars: Episode VIII - The Last Jedi (2017) — $1,332,698,830
- ☐ Jurassic World: Fallen Kingdom (2018) — $1,310,466,296
- ☐ Frozen (2013) — $1,281,508,100
- ☐ Beauty and the Beast (2017) — $1,273,576,220
- ☐ Incredibles 2 (2018) — $1,243,089,244
- ☐ The Fate of the Furious (2017) — $1,236,005,118
- ☐ Iron Man 3 (2013) — $1,214,811,252
- ☐ Minions (2015) — $1,159,444,662
- ☐ Captain America: Civil War (2016) — $1,153,337,496
- ☐ Aquaman (2018) — $1,148,485,886
- ☐ The Lord of the Rings: The Return of the King (2003) — $1,146,030,912
- ☐ Spider-Man: Far from Home (2019) — $1,131,927,996
- ☐ Captain Marvel (2019) — $1,128,462,972
- ☐ Transformers: Dark of the Moon (2011) — $1,123,794,079
- ☐ Skyfall (2012) — $1,108,569,499
- ☐ Transformers: Age of Extinction (2014) — $1,104,054,072
- ☐ The Dark Knight Rises (2012) — $1,081,142,612
- ☐ Joker (2019) — $1,074,419,384
- ☐ Star Wars: Episode IX - The Rise of Skywalker (2019) — $1,074,149,279

Whodunnit

"Whodunnit?", a question at the core of many stories. We love looking for clues, trying to work out the culprit before the big reveal. Can you guess whodunnit for this challenge?

Movie Watched:

_____

Directed By: Year Released:

_____   _____

Starring: Date Completed:

_____   _____

Your Review

_____

_____

_____

_____   ☆ ☆ ☆ ☆ ☆

Would you recommend it, and if so to who?

_____

_____

How closely did you guess the outcome?

_____

_____

These have all made $1b at the box office (at time of writing). Search online "top lifetime grosses" for a full list.

- ☐ After the Thin Man (1936)
- ☐ Rebecca (1940)
- ☐ The Maltese Falcon (1941)
- ☐ The Big Sleep (1946)
- ☐ Lady in the Lake (1947)
- ☐ The Man Who Knew Too Much (1956)
- ☐ North By Northwest (1959)
- ☐ Charade (1963)
- ☐ Klute (1971)
- ☐ The Long Goodbye (1973)
- ☐ The Last of Sheila (1973)
- ☐ Murder on the Orient Express (1974)
- ☐ Chinatown (1974)
- ☐ Blow Out (1981)
- ☐ Clue (1985)
- ☐ Who Framed Roger Rabbit? (1988)
- ☐ Primal Fear (1996)
- ☐ L.A. Confidential (1997)
- ☐ Zero Effect (1998)
- ☐ Memento (2000)
- ☐ Gosford Park (2001)
- ☐ Brick (2005)
- ☐ The Black Dahlia (2006)
- ☐ Zodiac (2007)
- ☐ Sherlock Holmes (2009)
- ☐ The Girl with the Dragon Tattoo (2011)
- ☐ The Girl on the Train (2016)
- ☐ The Nice Guys (2016)
- ☐ Hail, Caesar! (2016)
- ☐ Game Night (2018)
- ☐ A Simple Favor (2018)
- ☐ Knives Out (2019)

Titular Character

Some movies have a character's name right there in the title. For this challenge you should watch one of those, with one caveat, no nicknames allowed (e.g., Batman).

Movie Watched:

_____

Directed By: Year Released:

_____   _____

Starring: Date Completed:

_____   _____

Your Review

_____

_____

_____

_____   ☆ ☆ ☆ ☆ ☆

Would you recommend it, and if so to who?

_____

_____

Give the movie a new title, without referencing a character.

_____

_____

These movies all have a titular character. This list could easily be expanded to include biopics where the subjects name is in the title.

- ☐ Citizen Kane (1941)
- ☐ Bambi (1942)
- ☐ Dr. No (1962)
- ☐ Dr. Strangelove (1964)
- ☐ Goldfinger (1964)
- ☐ Cat Ballou (1965)
- ☐ Rosemary's Baby (1968)
- ☐ Cleopatra Jones (1973)
- ☐ Charley Varrick (1973)
- ☐ Robin Hood (1973)
- ☐ Barry Lyndon (1975)
- ☐ Carrie (1976)
- ☐ Rocky (1976)
- ☐ Mad Max (1979)
- ☐ Life of Brian (1979)
- ☐ Tron (1982)
- ☐ Amadeus (1984)
- ☐ Edward Scissorhands (1990)
- ☐ Barton Fink (1991)
- ☐ Thelma & Louise (1991)
- ☐ Forrest Gump (1994)
- ☐ Léon: The Professional (1994)
- ☐ Ed Wood (1994)
- ☐ Billy Madison (1995)
- ☐ Tommy Boy (1995)
- ☐ Babe (1995)
- ☐ Jerry Maguire (1996)
- ☐ Donnie Brasco (1997)
- ☐ Good Will Hunting (1997)
- ☐ Jackie Brown (1997)
- ☐ The Big Lebowski (1998)
- ☐ The Truman Show (1998)
- ☐ Saving Private Ryan (1998)
- ☐ Donnie Darko (2001)
- ☐ Amélie (2001)
- ☐ Antwone Fisher (2002)
- ☐ Napoleon Dynamite (2004)
- ☐ Pan's Labyrinth (2006)
- ☐ Michael Clayton (2007)
- ☐ Juno (2007)
- ☐ Lars and the Real Girl (2007)
- ☐ Fred Claus (2007)
- ☐ Speed Racer (2008)
- ☐ WALL·E (2008)
- ☐ Max Payne (2008)
- ☐ Mary and Max (2009)
- ☐ Coraline (2009)
- ☐ Dorian Gray (2009)
- ☐ Jennifer's Body (2009)
- ☐ Black Dynamite (2009)
- ☐ Harry Brown (2009)
- ☐ Sherlock Holmes (2009)
- ☐ Tamara Drewe (2010)
- ☐ Scott Pilgrim vs. the World (2010)
- ☐ Hugo (2011)
- ☐ Django Unchained (2012)
- ☐ Jack Reacher (2012)
- ☐ Inside Llewyn Davis (2013)
- ☐ Locke (2013)
- ☐ John Wick (2014)
- ☐ Paddington (2014)
- ☐ Mad Max: Fury Road (2015)
- ☐ Carol (2015)
- ☐ Steve Jobs (2015)
- ☐ Creed (2015)
- ☐ Moana (2016)
- ☐ Logan (2017)
- ☐ Cruella (2021)
- ☐ Luca (2021)

Stop Motion Animation

One of the many movie making techniques that CGI is slowing killing off is stop motion animation. Watch a movie featuring stop motion animation for this challenge.

Movie Watched:

_____

Directed By: Year Released:

_____   _____

Starring: Date Completed:

_____   _____

Your Review

_____

_____

_____

_____

_____   ☆ ☆ ☆ ☆ ☆

Would you recommend it, and if so to who?

_____

_____

Which do you prefer, CGI or stop motion animation?

_____

_____

We've combined stop motion animated movies with movies that feature stop motion sections for this list.

- ☐ King Kong (1933)
- ☐ Rudolph The Red Nosed Reindeer (1964)
- ☐ Mad Monster Party? (1967)
- ☐ Fantastic Planet (1973)
- ☐ The Evil Dead (1981)
- ☐ The Thing (1982)
- ☐ Beetlejuice (1988)
- ☐ A Grand Day Out (1989)
- ☐ The Nightmare Before Christmas (1993)
- ☐ The Wrong Trousers (1993)
- ☐ Mary and Max (2009)
- ☐ James and the Giant Peach (1996)
- ☐ Chicken Run (2000)
- ☐ Wallace & Gromit: The Curse of the Were-Rabbit (2005)
- ☐ Corpse Bride (2005)
- ☐ Fantastic Mr. Fox (2009)
- ☐ Coraline (2009)
- ☐ Toys in the Attic (2009)
- ☐ A Town Called Panic (2009)
- ☐ ParaNorman (2012)
- ☐ Frankenweenie (2012)
- ☐ The Pirates! In an Adventure with Scientists! (2012)
- ☐ The Boxtrolls (2014)
- ☐ Anomalisa (2015)
- ☐ Hell & Back (2015)
- ☐ Shaun the Sheep Movie (2015)
- ☐ Kubo and the Two Strings (2016)
- ☐ My Life as a Zucchini (2016)
- ☐ Isle of Dogs (2018)
- ☐ Early Man (2018)
- ☐ Missing Link (2019)
- ☐ A Shaun the Sheep Movie: Farmageddon (2019)

Set in a Location You Love

For this challenge we want you to watch a movie that is set in or contains a key scene from a location you love (e.g., country, city, settings, building).

Movie Watched:

_____

Directed By: Year Released:

_____   _____

Starring: Date Completed:

_____   _____

Your Review

_____

_____

_____

_____ ☆ ☆ ☆ ☆ ☆

Would you recommend it, and if so to who?

_____

_____

Which location did you choose and why?

_____

_____

You've got free rein on this challenge!

Pick a movie that features somewhere you like:
- Countries (U.S.A., Japan, England, Mexico, France)
- Cities (New York, London, Tokyo, Paris)
- Settings (City, Countryside, Beach)
- Vehicles (Submarines, Planes, Cars)
- Buildings (Warehouse, Restaurants, Office Blocks)
- Geographic Features (Waterfalls, mountains)
- Not Earth (The Moon, Mars, made up planets)

Use the space below to compile your own watchlist to complete this challenge.

☐
☐
☐
☐
☐
☐
☐
☐
☐
☐
☐
☐
☐
☐
☐
☐

Historical War

For this challenge you should watch a movie depiction of a real war that took place. While the plot can be about fictional characters (e.g., Saving Private Ryan) the war should be real.

Movie Watched:

_____

Directed By: Year Released:

_____   _____

Starring: Date Completed:

_____   _____

Your Review

_____

_____

_____

_____   ☆ ☆ ☆ ☆ ☆

Would you recommend it, and if so to who?

_____

_____

_____

Which war did you choose and why?

_____

_____

Below is a list of some of the greatest war movies as polled online.

- ☐ All Quiet on the Western Front (1930)
- ☐ Paths of Glory (1957)
- ☐ The Longest Day (1962)
- ☐ The Battle of Algiers (1966)
- ☐ Tora! Tora! Tora! (1970)
- ☐ A Bridge Too Far (1977)
- ☐ The Killing Fields (1984)
- ☐ Heartbreak Ridge (1986)
- ☐ Casualties of War (1989)
- ☐ Braveheart (1995)
- ☐ Saving Private Ryan (1998)
- ☐ The Thin Red Line (1998)
- ☐ Enemy at the Gates (2001)
- ☐ Pearl Harbor (2001)
- ☐ Black Hawk Down (2001)
- ☐ The Pianist (2002)
- ☐ Tae Guk Gi: The Brotherhood of War (2004)
- ☐ Troy (2004)
- ☐ Downfall (2004)
- ☐ Joyeux Noel (2005)
- ☐ Black Book (2006)
- ☐ Rescue Dawn (2006)
- ☐ Flags of Our Fathers (2006)
- ☐ Letters from Iwo Jima (2006)
- ☐ The Red Baron (2008)
- ☐ Fury (2014)
- ☐ American Sniper (2014)
- ☐ Unbroken (2014)
- ☐ Hacksaw Ridge (2016)
- ☐ 13 Hours: The Secret Soldiers of Benghazi (2016)
- ☐ Dunkirk (2017)
- ☐ 1917 (2019)

Stephen King Adaptation

Did you know Stephen King (at the time of writing) holds the world record most motion picture adaptations from a living author? Watch one for this challenge.

Movie Watched:

_____

Directed By: Year Released:

_____   _____

Starring: Date Completed:

_____   _____

Your Review

_____

_____

_____

_____

_____   ☆ ☆ ☆ ☆ ☆

Would you recommend it, and if so to who?

_____

_____

Have you/will you read the original story?

_____

_____

Here is a list of all of King's adaptations, including short stories. If nothing takes your fancy, then feel free to choose a different author.

- ☐ Carrie (1976)
- ☐ The Shining (1980)
- ☐ Cujo (1983)
- ☐ The Dead Zone (1983)
- ☐ Christine (1983)
- ☐ Children of the Corn (1984)
- ☐ Firestarter (1984)
- ☐ Cat's Eye (1985)
- ☐ Silver Bullet (1985)
- ☐ Maximum Overdrive (1986)
- ☐ Stand By Me (1986)
- ☐ The Running Man (1987)
- ☐ Creepshow 2 (1987)
- ☐ The Running Man (1987)
- ☐ Pet Sematary (1989)
- ☐ Graveyard Shift (1990)
- ☐ Tales from the Darkside: The Movie
- ☐ Misery (1990)
- ☐ The Lawnmower Man (1992)
- ☐ The Dark Half (1993)
- ☐ Needful Things (1991)
- ☐ The Shawshank Redemption (1994)
- ☐ Dolores Claiborne (1995)
- ☐ The Mangler (1995)
- ☐ Thinner (1996)
- ☐ The Night Flier (1997)
- ☐ Apt Pupil (1998)
- ☐ The Green Mile (1999)
- ☐ Hearts in Atlantis (2001)
- ☐ Dreamcatcher (2003)
- ☐ Secret Window (2004)
- ☐ Riding the Bullet (2004)
- ☐ 1408 (2007)
- ☐ The Mist (2007)
- ☐ Dolan's Cadillac (2009)
- ☐ Carrie (2013)
- ☐ Mercy (2014)
- ☐ A Good Marriage (2014)
- ☐ Cell (2016)
- ☐ The Dark Tower (2017)
- ☐ IT (2017)
- ☐ Gerald's Game (2017)
- ☐ 1922 (2017)
- ☐ Pet Sematary (2019)
- ☐ It Chapter Two (2019)
- ☐ In the Tall Grass (2019)
- ☐ Doctor Sleep (2019)

Jaw Dropping Cinematography

Cinematography is the art of photography and camerawork in filmmaking; the visuals on screen that make your jaw drop. Watch a movie with highly acclaimed visuals.

Movie Watched:

_____

Directed By: Year Released:

_____   _____

Starring: Date Completed:

_____   _____

Your Review

_____

_____

_____

_____   ☆ ☆ ☆ ☆ ☆

Would you recommend it, and if so to who?

_____

_____

Which movie's cinematography made your jaw drop?

_____

_____

For this challenge, an obvious starting point is choosing a winner of Best Cinematography at the Academy Awards (a small handful of which we've listed below). However, everyone has an opinion, and the internet is where those opinions are voiced! We're sure you can find an article online recommending other movies with stellar visuals.

- ☐ Tabu (1931)
- ☐ Shanghai Express (1932)
- ☐ Cleopatra (1934)
- ☐ Wuthering Heights (1939)
- ☐ Gone with the Wind (1939)
- ☐ Rebecca (1940)
- ☐ Blood and Sand (1941)
- ☐ Mrs. Miniver (1942)
- ☐ The Yearling (1946)
- ☐ Great Expectations (1946)
- ☐ Black Narcissus (1947)
- ☐ Joan of Arc (1948)
- ☐ The Third Man (1949)
- ☐ King Solomon's Mines (1950)
- ☐ The Quiet Man (1952)
- ☐ From Here to Eternity (1953)
- ☐ On the Waterfront (1954)
- ☐ To Catch a Thief (1955)
- ☐ The Bridge on the River Kwai (1957)
- ☐ Gigi (1958)
- ☐ Ben-Hur (1959)
- ☐ Spartacus (1960)
- ☐ The Hustler (1961)
- ☐ West Side Story (1961)
- ☐ The Longest Day (1962)
- ☐ Lawrence of Arabia (1962)

- ☐ Cleopatra (1963)
- ☐ Doctor Zhivago (1965)
- ☐ Bonnie and Clyde (1967)
- ☐ Barry Lyndon (1975)
- ☐ Close Encounters of the Third Kind (1977)
- ☐ Apocalypse Now (1979)
- ☐ Gandhi (1982)
- ☐ Out of Africa (1985)
- ☐ The Last Emperor (1987)
- ☐ Glory (1989)
- ☐ Dances with Wolves (1990)
- ☐ Legends of the Fall (1994)
- ☐ Braveheart (1995)
- ☐ The English Patient (1996)
- ☐ Titanic (1997)
- ☐ Saving Private Ryan (1998)
- ☐ Road to Perdition (2002)
- ☐ Memoirs of a Geisha (2005)
- ☐ Pan's Labyrinth (2006)
- ☐ There Will Be Blood (2007)
- ☐ Hugo (2011)
- ☐ Life of Pi (2012)
- ☐ The Revenant (2015)
- ☐ La La Land (2016)
- ☐ Blade Runner (2049 (2017)
- ☐ 1917 (2019)

An Obsession

Movies about obsessions can excite and scare us in equal measures. Whether an author trying to finish their work, or a crazed fan re-writing it, watch a movie about an obsession.

Movie Watched:

_____

Directed By: Year Released:

_____   _____

Starring: Date Completed:

_____   _____

Your Review

_____

_____

_____

_____   ☆ ☆ ☆ ☆ ☆

Would you recommend it, and if so to who?

_____

_____

What's your obsession, which actor would portray it best?

_____

_____

The obvious place to start with obsession-based movies is the unrequited love aka "the stalker" movie, some of which are on the list below.

- ☐ Lolita (1962)
- ☐ The Conversation (1974)
- ☐ Taxi Driver (1976)
- ☐ Close Encounters of the Third Kind (1977)
- ☐ The Shining (1980)
- ☐ The Fan (1981)
- ☐ Fatal Attraction (1987)
- ☐ Misery (1990)
- ☐ Sleeping With the Enemy (1991)
- ☐ Single White Female (1992)
- ☐ The Hand The Rocks the Cradle (1992)
- ☐ The Crush (1993)
- ☐ Muriel's Wedding (1994)
- ☐ Fear (1996)
- ☐ Being John Malkovich (1999)
- ☐ Superstar (1999)
- ☐ The Cell (2000)
- ☐ Amélie (2001)
- ☐ Adaptation (2002)
- ☐ The Rules of Attraction (2002)
- ☐ Catch Me If You Can (2002)
- ☐ The Fountain (2006)
- ☐ Black Swan (2010)
- ☐ Whiplash (2014)
- ☐ Nightcrawler (2014)
- ☐ Gone Girl (2014)
- ☐ Fifty Shades of Grey (2015)
- ☐ The Girl on the Train (2016)
- ☐ I, Tonya (2017)
- ☐ Mainstream (2020)

Powerful Endings

Arguably of the most memorable movies come with an ending that hits you out of the blue, that you can't stop thinking about. Watch one for this challenge.

Movie Watched:

_____

Directed By: Year Released:

_____   _____

Starring: Date Completed:

_____   _____

Your Review

_____

_____

_____

_____

_____ ☆ ☆ ☆ ☆ ☆

Would you recommend it, and if so to who?

_____

_____

Which movie endings stick out in your mind?

_____

_____

No spoilers, but these are some that blew us away.

- ☐ The Cabinet of Dr. Caligari (1920)
- ☐ City Lights (1931)
- ☐ The Great Dictator (1940)
- ☐ Citizen Kane (1941)
- ☐ Casablanca (1942)
- ☐ Bicycle Thieves (1948)
- ☐ Sunset Boulevard (1950)
- ☐ Roman Holiday (1953)
- ☐ The Killing (1956)
- ☐ The Bridge on the River Kwai (1957)
- ☐ Vertigo (1958)
- ☐ Eyes Without a Face (1960)
- ☐ Psycho (1960)
- ☐ The Good, the Bad and the Ugly (1966)
- ☐ Planet of the Apes (1968)
- ☐ 2001: A Space Odyssey (1968)
- ☐ if.... (1968)
- ☐ A Clockwork Orange (1971)
- ☐ The Wicker Man (1973)
- ☐ The Conversation (1974)
- ☐ Dog Day Afternoon (1975)
- ☐ Taxi Driver (1976)
- ☐ Carrie (1976)
- ☐ The Thing (1982)
- ☐ Back to the Future (1985)
- ☐ The Vanishing (1988)
- ☐ Jacob's Ladder (1990)
- ☐ The Silence of the Lambs (1991)
- ☐ Se7en (1995)
- ☐ The Usual Suspects (1995)
- ☐ Funny Games (1997)
- ☐ Audition (1999)
- ☐ The Blair Witch Project (1999)
- ☐ The Sixth Sense (1999)
- ☐ Magnolia (1999)
- ☐ Memento (2000)
- ☐ Requiem for a Dream (2000)
- ☐ Unbreakable (2000)
- ☐ Donnie Darko (2001)
- ☐ Vanilla Sky (2001)
- ☐ Oldboy (2003)
- ☐ Dead Man's Shoes (2004)
- ☐ Tae Guk Gi: The Brotherhood of War (2004)
- ☐ The Mist (2007)
- ☐ There Will Be Blood (2007)
- ☐ The Wrestler (2008)
- ☐ Eden Lake (2008)
- ☐ Orphan (2009)
- ☐ 3 Idiots (2009)
- ☐ Four Lions (2010)
- ☐ I Saw the Devil (2010)
- ☐ Snowpiercer (2013)
- ☐ Prisoners (2013)
- ☐ Enemy (2013)
- ☐ Whiplash (2014)
- ☐ Birdman or (The Unexpected Virtue of Ignorance) (2014)
- ☐ Gone Girl (2014)
- ☐ Phantom Thread (2017)

The Same Age as You

For this challenge we want you to watch a movie released the year you were born. Any genre, just choose something the same age as you.

Movie Watched:

_____

Directed By: Year Released:

_____   _____

Starring: Date Completed:

_____   _____

Your Review

_____

_____

_____

_____   ☆ ☆ ☆ ☆ ☆

Would you recommend it, and if so to who?

_____

_____

The best movies released the year you were born are:

_____

_____

We obviously can't make any suggestions of what to watch here. Instead, we've left some space below for you to populate your own watchlist, once you've looked up online what movies were released the same year you were born.

☐

☐

☐

☐

☐

☐

☐

☐

☐

☐

☐

☐

☐

☐

☐

☐

☐

☐

☐

☐

☐

☐

☐

LGBTQIA+

Over recent years LGBTQIA+ movies have been brought more into the mainstream, and even dominated awards shows. Watch one for this challenge.

Movie Watched:

_____

Directed By: Year Released:

_____   _____

Starring: Date Completed:

_____   _____

Your Review

_____

_____

_____

_____   ☆ ☆ ☆ ☆ ☆

Would you recommend it, and if so to who?

_____

_____

Were LGBTQIA+ movies on your radar before this?

_____

_____

Search online for recommendations, or watch one of ours:

- ☐ Dog Day Afternoon (1975)
- ☐ The Rocky Horror Picture Show (1975)
- ☐ La Cage aux Folles (1978)
- ☐ Cruising (1980)
- ☐ My Own Private Idaho (1991)
- ☐ Philadelphia (1993)
- ☐ The Adventures of Priscilla, Queen of the Desert (1994)
- ☐ To Wong Foo, Thanks for Everything! Julie Newmar (1995)
- ☐ Showgirls (1995)
- ☐ The Birdcage (1996)
- ☐ Bound (1996)
- ☐ Chasing Amy (1997)
- ☐ In & Out (1997)
- ☐ Boogie Nights (1997)
- ☐ Gods and Monsters (1998)
- ☐ Gia (1998)
- ☐ But I'm a Cheerleader (1999)
- ☐ Hedwig and the Angry Inch (2001)
- ☐ Kissing Jessica Stein (2001)
- ☐ Mulholland Drive (2001)
- ☐ Far from Heaven (2002)
- ☐ The Hours (2002)
- ☐ Monster (2003)
- ☐ Brokeback Mountain (2005)
- ☐ Rent (2005)
- ☐ Transamerica (2005)
- ☐ Dogtooth (2009)
- ☐ Tomboy (2011)
- ☐ Kill Your Darlings (2013)
- ☐ Blue Is the Warmest Color (2013)
- ☐ Dallas Buyers Club (2013)
- ☐ The Imitation Game (2014)
- ☐ Pride (2014)
- ☐ Tangerine (2015)
- ☐ Carol (2015)
- ☐ The Danish Girl (2015)
- ☐ The Handmaiden (2016)
- ☐ Moonlight (2016)
- ☐ Below Her Mouth (2016)
- ☐ Call Me by Your Name (2017)
- ☐ Battle of the Sexes (2017)
- ☐ Disobedience (2017)
- ☐ The Greatest Showman (2017)
- ☐ Assassination Nation (2018)
- ☐ The Miseducation of Cameron Post (2018)
- ☐ Love, Simon (2018)
- ☐ Climax (2018)
- ☐ Girl (2018)
- ☐ The Favourite (2018)
- ☐ Boy Erased (2018)
- ☐ Can You Ever Forgive Me? (2018)
- ☐ The Perfection (2018)
- ☐ Bohemian Rhapsody (2018)
- ☐ Booksmart (2019)
- ☐ Rocketman (2019)
- ☐ Portrait of a Lady on Fire (2019)
- ☐ Ammonite (2020)

The Title is a Question

To complete this challenge, we want you to watch a movie where the title of the movie is a question, although it doesn't have to have a question mark in the title...

Movie Watched:

_____

Directed By: Year Released:

_____   _____

Starring: Date Completed:

_____   _____

Your Review

_____

_____

_____

_____

_____   ☆ ☆ ☆ ☆ ☆

Would you recommend it, and if so to who?

_____

_____

If the title of your biopic was a question, what would it be?

_____

_____

There is a reason some of these don't have a question mark at the end of the title. There is a superstition in Hollywood that have a question mark in the title hurts the box office.

- ☐ Where Do We Go From Here? (1945)
- ☐ Who's Got the Action? (1962)
- ☐ What Ever Happened to Baby Jane? (1962)
- ☐ Who's Afraid of Virginia Woolf? (1966)
- ☐ Is Paris Burning? (1966)
- ☐ Guess Who's Coming to Dinner (1967)
- ☐ They Shoot Horses, Don't They? (1969)
- ☐ Whoever Slew Auntie Roo? (1971)
- ☐ Who Can Kill a Child? (1976)
- ☐ Casual Sex? (1988)
- ☐ Who Framed Roger Rabbit (1988)
- ☐ Who's Harry Crumb? (1989)
- ☐ What About Bob? (1991)
- ☐ What's Eating Gilbert Grape? (1993)
- ☐ What's Love Got to Do with it (1993)
- ☐ Car 54, Where Are You? (1994)
- ☐ Why Do Fools Fall In Love (1998)
- ☐ Who Am I? (1998)
- ☐ Dude, Where's My Car? (2000)
- ☐ O Brother, Where Art Thou? (2000)
- ☐ Who Killed Bambi? (2003)
- ☐ Shall We Dance? (2004)
- ☐ When Will I Be Loved (2004)
- ☐ Are We There Yet? (2005)
- ☐ When Did You Last See Your Father? (2007)
- ☐ What Just Happened (2008)
- ☐ Did You Hear About the Morgans? (2009)
- ☐ How Do You Know (2010)
- ☐ What's Your Number? (2011)
- ☐ Why Him? (2016)
- ☐ Won't You Be My Neighbor? (2018)

Film Noir

The term "Film Noir" comes from French critic Nino Frank to describe movies with an atmosphere of pessimism, anxiety, and fatalism. Choose one for this challenge.

Movie Watched:

_____

Directed By: Year Released:

_____   _____

Starring: Date Completed:

_____   _____

Your Review

_____

_____

_____

_____

_____   ☆ ☆ ☆ ☆ ☆

Would you recommend it, and if so to who?

_____

_____

_____

Do you consider film noir a genre, or a style of movie?

_____

_____

We've listed below some essential film noir. There are hundreds of excellent choices, including more modern movies filmed in colour if that's your thing. Have a look online for more recommendations.

- ☐ The Maltese Falcon (1941)
- ☐ Laura (1944)
- ☐ Christmas Holiday (1944)
- ☐ Shadow of a Doubt (1943)
- ☐ Double Indemnity (1944)
- ☐ Murder, My Sweet (1944)
- ☐ Scarlet Street (1945)
- ☐ Fallen Angel (1945)
- ☐ Mildred Pierce (1945)
- ☐ Detour (1945)
- ☐ Hangover Square (1945)
- ☐ Cornered (1945)
- ☐ My Name Is Julia Ross (1945)
- ☐ The Postman Always Rings Twice (1946)
- ☐ The Killers (1946)
- ☐ The Big Sleep (1946)
- ☐ Gilda (1946)
- ☐ Brute Force (1947)
- ☐ Body and Soul (1947)
- ☐ Born to Kill (1947)
- ☐ Nightmare Alley (1947)
- ☐ Dead Reckoning (1947)
- ☐ They Won't Believe Me (1947)
- ☐ Nora Prentiss (1947)
- ☐ Out of the Past (1947)
- ☐ The Lady from Shanghai (1947)
- ☐ D.O.A. (1949)
- ☐ Champion (1949)
- ☐ The Set-Up (1949)
- ☐ Criss Cross (1949)
- ☐ The Reckless Moment (1949)
- ☐ Gun Crazy (1950)
- ☐ In a Lonely Place (1950)
- ☐ Night and the City (1950)
- ☐ Sunset Boulevard (1950)
- ☐ Ace in the Hole (1951)
- ☐ The Narrow Margin (1952)
- ☐ Angel Face (1953)
- ☐ The Big Heat (1953)
- ☐ The Hitch-Hiker (1953)
- ☐ Strangers on a Train (1951)
- ☐ Human Desire (1954)
- ☐ Kiss Me Deadly (1955)
- ☐ The Killing (1956)
- ☐ Beyond a Reasonable Doubt (1956)
- ☐ Sweet Smell of Success (1957)
- ☐ Touch of Evil (1958)
- ☐ The Lineup (1958)
- ☐ Cape Fear (1962)

A Title at Least 5 Words Long

We love a long movie title, the more ridiculous the better. For this challenge watch a movie with a title that contains at least 5 words.

Movie Watched:

_____

Directed By: Year Released:

_____   _____

Starring: Date Completed:

_____   _____

Your Review

_____

_____

_____

_____   ☆ ☆ ☆ ☆ ☆

Would you recommend it, and if so to who?

_____

_____

Using only 1 word, give the movie a new title:

_____

_____

Due to the title lengths, we've only included a few recommendations here, but you can find plenty online.

- ☐ Mr. Smith Goes to Washington (1939)
- ☐ The Postman Always Rings Twice (1946)
- ☐ The Day the Earth Stood Still (1951)
- ☐ It's a Mad, Mad, Mad, Mad World (1963)
- ☐ Dr. Strangelove or: How I Learned to Stop Worrying and Love the Bomb (1964)
- ☐ Once Upon a Time in the West (1968)
- ☐ Live Like a Cop, Die Like a Man (1976)
- ☐ The Man Who Fell to Earth (1976)
- ☐ An American Werewolf in London (1981)
- ☐ Throw Momma From the Train (1987)
- ☐ So I Married an Axe Murderer (1993)
- ☐ 10 Things I Hate About You (1999)
- ☐ O Brother, Where Art Thou? (2000)
- ☐ Eternal Sunshine of the Spotless Mind (2004)
- ☐ The Life Aquatic with Steve Zissou (2004)
- ☐ The Assassination of Jesse James by the Coward Robert Ford (2007)
- ☐ How to Train Your Dragon (2010)
- ☐ We Need to Talk About Kevin (2011)
- ☐ The 100 Year-Old Man Who Climbed Out the Window and Disappeared (2013)
- ☐ What We Do in the Shadows (2014)
- ☐ Scouts Guide to the Zombie Apocalypse (2015)
- ☐ Popstar: Never Stop Never Stopping (2016)
- ☐ Miss Peregrine's Home for Peculiar Children (2016)
- ☐ The Killing of a Sacred Deer (2017)
- ☐ Film Stars Don't Die in Liverpool (2017)
- ☐ I Want to Eat Your Pancreas (2018)
- ☐ The Last Black Man in San Francisco (2019)
- ☐ Birds of Prey (and the Fantabulous Emancipation of One Harley Quinn) (2020)
- ☐ Barb & Star Go to Vista Del Mar (2021)

Doesn't Take Place on Earth

One thing we all have in common is we all live on Earth. To complete this challenge, watch a movie that doesn't take place here i.e., on another planet or spaceship.

Movie Watched:

_____

Directed By: Year Released:

_____   _____

Starring: Date Completed:

_____   _____

Your Review

_____

_____

_____

_____

_____   ☆ ☆ ☆ ☆ ☆

Would you recommend it, and if so to who?

_____

_____

Was it set on another planet or a spaceship?

_____

_____

A small selection of movies set in outer space or on alternate planets for your perusal.

- ☐ Destination Moon 1950)
- ☐ Forbidden Planet (1956)
- ☐ Planet of the Vampires (1965)
- ☐ 2001: A Space Odyssey (1968)
- ☐ Barbarella (1968)
- ☐ Solaris (1972)
- ☐ Fantastic Planet (1973)
- ☐ Starcrash (1978)
- ☐ Alien (1979)
- ☐ The Black Hole (1979)
- ☐ Flash Gordon (1980)
- ☐ Outland (1981)
- ☐ The Last Starfighter (1984)
- ☐ Dune (1984, 2021)
- ☐ 2010 (1984)
- ☐ Explorers (1985)
- ☐ Enemy Mine (1985)
- ☐ The Transformers: The Movie (1986)
- ☐ Spaceballs (1987)
- ☐ The Dark Side of The Moon (1990)
- ☐ Total Recall (1990)
- ☐ Stargate (1994)
- ☐ The Fifth Element (1997)
- ☐ Contact (1997)
- ☐ Event Horizon (1997)
- ☐ Starship Troopers (1997)
- ☐ Dark City (1998)
- ☐ Galaxy Quest (1999)
- ☐ Supernova (2000)
- ☐ Pitch Black (2000)
- ☐ Mission to Mars (2000)
- ☐ Red Planet (2000)
- ☐ Cowboy Bebop: The Movie (2001)
- ☐ The Chronicles of Riddick (2004)
- ☐ The Hitchhiker's Guide to the Galaxy (2005)
- ☐ Sunshine (2007)
- ☐ WALL·E (2008)
- ☐ Moon (2009)
- ☐ Virtuality (2009)
- ☐ Pandorum (2009)
- ☐ Avatar (2009)
- ☐ Apollo 18 (2011)
- ☐ Lockout (2012)
- ☐ Europa Report (2013)
- ☐ Gravity (2013)
- ☐ Interstellar (2014)
- ☐ Guardians of the Galaxy (2014)
- ☐ The Martian (2015)
- ☐ Valerian and the City of a Thousand Planets (2017)
- ☐ Ad Astra (2019)
- ☐ Captain Marvel (2019)

25, 50 or 100 Year Anniversary

For this challenge we want you to celebrate a movies' anniversary. Watch something that was released 25, 50 or 100 years ago.

Movie Watched:

_____

Directed By: Year Released:

_____   _____

Starring: Date Completed:

_____   _____

Your Review

_____

_____

_____

_____

_____   ☆ ☆ ☆ ☆ ☆

Would you recommend it, and if so to who?

_____

_____

_____

How old was the movie you watched?

_____

_____

We can't make any suggestions of what to watch here as we don't know what year you're reading this. Instead, we've left some space below for you to populate your own watchlist once you've looked up some movie anniversaries.

☐
☐
☐
☐
☐
☐
☐
☐
☐
☐
☐
☐
☐
☐
☐
☐
☐
☐
☐
☐
☐
☐

Set in the Winter

If you started these challenges in the New Year, and have been doing a challenge a week, it should now be winter. Either way, watch a winter themed movie for this challenge.

Movie Watched:

_____

Directed By: Year Released:

_____   _____

Starring: Date Completed:

_____   _____

Your Review

_____

_____

_____

_____

_____   ☆ ☆ ☆ ☆ ☆

Would you recommend it, and if so to who?

_____

_____

_____

Which is you're preferred season for a movie to take place?

_____

_____

Wrap up warm with one of these winter themed movies to keep you company, or search for recommendations online.

- ☐ The 39 Steps (1935)
- ☐ It's a Wonderful Life (1946)
- ☐ The Spy Who Came in from the Cold (1965)
- ☐ Doctor Zhivago (1965)
- ☐ Tokyo Drifter (1966)
- ☐ Le Samouraï (1967)
- ☐ Jeremiah Johnson (1972)
- ☐ The Godfather: Part II (1974)
- ☐ The Little Girl Who Lives Down the Lane (1976)
- ☐ The Shining (1980)
- ☐ Ghost Story (1981)
- ☐ The Thing (1982)
- ☐ Gremlins (1984)
- ☐ Running Scared (1986)
- ☐ Dead of Winter (1987)
- ☐ Planes, Trains and Automobiles (1987)
- ☐ Die Hard (1988)
- ☐ Misery (1990)
- ☐ Dreams (1990)
- ☐ Edward Scissorhands (1990)
- ☐ Batman Returns (1992)
- ☐ Groundhog Day (1993)
- ☐ Zero Kelvin (1995)
- ☐ Fargo (1996)
- ☐ The Long Kiss Goodnight (1996)
- ☐ The Ice Storm (1997)
- ☐ Insomnia (1997)
- ☐ Eyes Wide Shut (1999)
- ☐ Moulin Rouge! (2001)
- ☐ One Hour Photo (2002)
- ☐ Road to Perdition (2002)
- ☐ Eternal Sunshine of the Spotless Mind (2004)
- ☐ Kiss Kiss Bang Bang (2005)
- ☐ The Holiday (2006)
- ☐ Reign Over Me (2007)
- ☐ 30 Days of Night (2007)
- ☐ Let the Right One In (2008)
- ☐ Where the Wild Things Are (2009)
- ☐ Scott Pilgrim vs. the World (2010)
- ☐ Black Swan (2010)
- ☐ Winter's Bone (2010)
- ☐ The Grey (2011)
- ☐ Hugo (2011)
- ☐ The Girl with the Dragon Tattoo (2011)
- ☐ Inside Llewyn Davis (2013)
- ☐ Nebraska (2013)
- ☐ Snowpiercer (2013)
- ☐ Prisoners (2013)
- ☐ The Grand Budapest Hotel (2014)
- ☐ A Most Violent Year (2014)
- ☐ Winter Sleep (2014)
- ☐ The Revenant (2015)
- ☐ Carol (2015)
- ☐ Spotlight (2015)
- ☐ The Hateful Eight (2015)

Biggest Return on Investment

For this challenge we're looking at movies that had a small budget, and combined with massive ticket sales, had an enormous return on investment.

Movie Watched:

_____

Directed By: Year Released:

_____   _____

Starring: Date Completed:

_____   _____

Your Review

_____

_____

_____

_____

_____   ☆ ☆ ☆ ☆ ☆

Would you recommend it, and if so to who?

_____

_____

Do you have a movie idea which would cost little to make?

_____

_____

These all made a huge profit. Choose one of these or look online for more examples.

		Budget	ROI
☐	Deep Throat (1972)	$25,000	90,014%
☐	Facing the Giants (2006)	$38,451	38,451%
☐	Paranormal Activity (2007)	$450,000	19,761%
☐	Fireproof (2008)	$500,000	11,319%
☐	The Texas Chainsaw Massacre (1974)	$140,000	10,018%
☐	The Gallows (2015)	$100,000	6,798%
☐	Eraserhead (1977)	$100,000	4,553%
☐	An Inconvenient Truth (2006)	$1,000,000	4,542%
☐	The Big Parade (1925)	$245,000	4,396%
☐	The Devil Inside (2012)	$1,000,000	3,642%
☐	A Charlie Brown Christmas (1965)	$150,000	3,438%
☐	Peter Pan (1953)	$4,000,000	3,394%
☐	Cat People (1942)	$134,000	3,330%
☐	Waiting… (2005)	$1,125,000	3,111%
☐	God's Not Dead (2014)	$1,150,000	3,091%
☐	Grease (1978)	$6,000,000	2,969%
☐	High School Musical (2006)	$4,200,000	2,843%
☐	Star Wars: A New Hope (1977)	$11,000,000	2,563%
☐	Paranormal Activity 2 (2010)	$3,000,000	2,474%
☐	Insidious (2011)	$1,500,000	2,246%
☐	Split (2011)	$5,000,000	2,077%
☐	Intouchables (2012)	$10,800,000	2,043%
☐	Young Frankenstein (1974)	$2,800,000	1,954%
☐	It's a Wonderful Life (1946)	$3,180,000	1,804%
☐	Reservoir Dogs (1992)	$1,200,000	1,771%
☐	Jaws (1975)	$12,000,000	1,755%
☐	Annabelle (2014)	$6,500,000	1,408%
☐	Beauty and the Beast (1991)	$20,000,000	1,340%
☐	The Kings Speech (2010)	$15,000,000	1,209%
☐	Magic Mike (2012)	$7,000,000	1,181%

One Actor, Multiple Roles

Let's celebrate actors that go above and beyond and play more than one role in a movie. Watch a movie with an actor taking on multiple roles.

Movie Watched:

_____

Directed By: Year Released:

_____   _____

Starring: Date Completed:

_____   _____

Your Review

_____

_____

_____

_____

_____ ☆ ☆ ☆ ☆ ☆

Would you recommend it, and if so to who?

_____

_____

Which actor played multiple roles, and how many was it?

_____

_____

At the time of writing, Eddie Murphy has played multiple roles in 7 different movies! We included just 1 of those here:

- ☐ The Wizard of Oz (1939)
- ☐ The Parent Trap (1961)
- ☐ The Great Dictator (1940)
- ☐ The Nutty Professor (1963)
- ☐ Dr. Strangelove or: How I Learned to Stop Worrying and Love the Bomb (1964)
- ☐ Mary Poppins (1964)
- ☐ Sisters (1972)
- ☐ Blazing Saddles (1974)
- ☐ Tron (1982)
- ☐ Spaceballs (1987)
- ☐ Coming to America (1988)
- ☐ Back to the Future Part II (1989)
- ☐ Double Impact (1991)
- ☐ Twin Dragons (1992)
- ☐ Clerks (1994)
- ☐ From Dusk Till Dawn (1996)
- ☐ Mars Attacks! (1996)
- ☐ Austin Powers: International Man of Mystery (1997)
- ☐ Mulholland Drive (2001)
- ☐ Harry Potter and the Philosopher's Stone (2001)
- ☐ Adaptation. (2002)
- ☐ Sin City (2005)
- ☐ The Island (2005)
- ☐ The Social Network (2010)
- ☐ Cloud Atlas (2012)
- ☐ The Double (2013)
- ☐ Enemy (2013)
- ☐ Legend (2015)
- ☐ Suspiria (2018)
- ☐ An American Pickle (2020)

Based on a Video Game

Nowadays movies and games go hand in hand, with them often being based on each or developed at the same time. Watch a movie based on a video game for this challenge.

Movie Watched:

_____

Directed By: Year Released:

_____   _____

Starring: Date Completed:

_____   _____

Your Review

_____

_____

_____

_____   ☆ ☆ ☆ ☆ ☆

Would you recommend it, and if so to who?

_____

_____

Have you played the game? If not, were you aware of it?

_____

_____

We've left sequels off this list, but even then, this list is far from complete. Choose one of these or ask friends for ideas.

- ☐ Super Mario Bros. (1993)
- ☐ Double Dragon (1994)
- ☐ Street Fighter (1994)
- ☐ Mortal Kombat (1995)
- ☐ Wing Commander (1999)
- ☐ Pokémon: The Movie (1999)
- ☐ Lara Croft: Tomb Raider (2001)
- ☐ Final Fantasy: The Spirits Within (2001)
- ☐ Resident Evil (2002)
- ☐ House of the Dead (2003)
- ☐ Alone in the Dark (2005)
- ☐ Doom (2005)
- ☐ Silent Hill (2006)
- ☐ DOA: Dead or Alive (2006)
- ☐ In the Name of the King: A Dungeon Siege Tale (2007)
- ☐ Hitman (2007)
- ☐ Far Cry (2008)
- ☐ Max Payne (2008)
- ☐ TEKKEN (2010)
- ☐ Prince of Persia: The Sands of Time (2010)
- ☐ Need for Speed (2014)
- ☐ Pixels (2015)
- ☐ The Angry Birds Movie (2016)
- ☐ Warcraft (2016)
- ☐ Assassin's Creed (2016)
- ☐ Tomb Raider (2018)
- ☐ Rampage (2018)
- ☐ Pokémon Detective Pikachu (2019)
- ☐ Sonic the Hedgehog (2020)
- ☐ Monster Hunter (2020)
- ☐ Werewolves Within (2021)
- ☐ Uncharted (2022)

A Christmas Movie

There's been a debate amongst movie fans since its release in July 1988, is Die Hard a Christmas movie? Watch whatever movie you consider a Christmas movie.

Movie Watched:

_____

Directed By: Year Released:

_____   _____

Starring: Date Completed:

_____   _____

Your Review

_____

_____

_____

_____

☆ ☆ ☆ ☆ ☆

Would you recommend it, and if so to who?

_____

_____

Do you consider Die Hard (1988) a Christmas movie?

_____

_____

We're all familiar with Christmas movies like Home Alone, Elf, and Miracle on 34th Street. This list contains alternative Christmas movies you may not have considered.

- ☐ Silent Night, Bloody Night (1972)
- ☐ Black Christmas (1974)
- ☐ The Silent Partner (1978)
- ☐ Christmas Evil (1980)
- ☐ Trading Places (1983)
- ☐ Merry Christmas, Mr. Lawrence (1983)
- ☐ Silent Night, Deadly Night (1984)
- ☐ Gremlins (1984)
- ☐ Lethal Weapon (1987)
- ☐ Die Hard (1988)
- ☐ Metropolitan (1990)
- ☐ The Long Kiss Goodnight (1996)
- ☐ L.A. Confidential (1997)
- ☐ Eyes Wide Shut (1999)
- ☐ American Psycho (2000)
- ☐ Bad Santa (2003)
- ☐ Kiss Kiss Bang Bang (2005)
- ☐ Black Christmas (2006)
- ☐ In Bruges (2008)
- ☐ Rare Exports: A Christmas Tale (2010)
- ☐ Prometheus (2012)
- ☐ Iron Man 3 (2013)
- ☐ Carol (2015)
- ☐ Krampus (2015)
- ☐ Tangerine (2015)
- ☐ The Night Before (2015)
- ☐ Better Watch Out (2016)
- ☐ Anna and the Apocalypse (2017)
- ☐ Office Christmas Party (2016)
- ☐ Godmothered (2020)
- ☐ Happiest Season (2020)

Released This Year

We've saved probably the easiest challenge for last. Simply watch a movie that was released this year.

Movie Watched:

_____

Directed By: Year Released:

_____   _____

Starring: Date Completed:

_____   _____

Your Review

_____

_____

_____

_____ ☆ ☆ ☆ ☆ ☆

Would you recommend it, and if so to who?

_____

_____

Why did you choose this movie?

_____

_____

We can't provide any suggestions or recommendations for this challenge, as it depends on the year that you're reading this.

Use the space below to compile your own watchlist to complete this challenge.

☐

☐

☐

☐

☐

☐

☐

☐

☐

☐

☐

☐

☐

☐

☐

☐

☐

☐

☐

☐

☐

☐

Printed in Great Britain
by Amazon